SCREEN
RESOLUTION

BRETT LEE
with David Morris

First Published in Australia by Aurora House
www.aurorahouse.com.au

This edition published 2017
Copyright © Brett Lee and David Morris 2017
Typesetting: Chameleon Print Design
Cover design, typesetting: Chameleon Print Design

The right of Brett Lee and David Morris to be identified as Authors of
the Work has been asserted in accordance with the Copyright, Designs
and Patents Act 1988.

ISBN number: 9780987617620 (paperback)

National Library of Australia Cataloguing-in-Publication entry
(paperback)
Creator: Lee, Brett, author.
Title: Screen resolution / Brett Lee with David Morris.
ISBN: 9780987617620 (paperback)
Subjects: Internet--Safety measures.
Internet and children--Safety measures.
Web sites for children.
Other Creators/Contributors:
Morris, David, author.

This book is dedicated to the future of families everywhere, not the least our own who mean the world to us...

Brett's family — Di, Tom, Nick, Rosie, and Josh

and

David's family — Jess, Candice, Brenton, Chantelle, and David (Junior)

Acknowledgements

Thanks to all who contributed resources, insights, and expertise:

For use of your offices for long hours of work on the book — Sedgman Pty Ltd and Councillor David Morrison, Ipswich City

For your priceless reviews and feedback — Paul Andrews, Paxton Booth, Kerry Davies, Kim Dorr, Jade Harrison, Jaclyn King, David Le Page, Francis Meyer, Anne Moffit, Anthony Morgan, and Ruth Shelling

For your kind foreword — Commissioner Ken Moroney

For putting the polish on the message that everyone needs to hear — publisher Linda Lycett and assistant/editor Sarah Vogler at Aurora House, and designer Luke Harris of Chameleon Print Design.

Contents

About the Authors

Brett Lee

A former undercover internet detective and police officer of twenty-two years, Brett is passionate about informing parents of the online risks to their children. Brett came face to face with computer predators and learnt their ploys while pretending to be a young person online. In these cyber playgrounds of the world's teenagers and children, he found predators preying on the vulnerable. Invariably, their targets were children and young people without adult supervision.

'I had a unique opportunity to see these offenders through the eyes of a child and combat them with the mind of an adult,' Brett, a father of four, says.

Brett's involvement led to the arrest of scores of alleged offenders over a five-year period. He also took part in early collaborative ties between Australian and United States (US) law enforcement agencies battling this online epidemic.

Brett subsequently founded training company INESS (Internet Education and Safety Services), which has now evolved into a speaking, face to face, and online training and resource business, Internet Safe Education.

(http://www.internetsafeeducation.com).

David Morris

David and Brett were boyhood friends who reconnected after thirty years of pursuing their own careers — David as a journalist, with publications including the *Melbourne Herald-Sun*, *Burnie Advocate*, and *Queensland Times*, and as a communications consultant to the government and corporate sector. Also a father of four, David identifies with Brett's vision to make the internet a safe playground. This book is the synergy of two friends.

Foreword

"There can be no keener revelation of a society's soul than the way in which it treats its children."
Nelson Mandela.

There are many quotes to be found about the importance and value of children in our society. Today, they are our future and in order to make that future one of hope and certainty, we as a society, as parents, grandparents, and families, must strive to ensure that the future of our children is founded in trust and built on safety.

Brett Lee, an experienced undercover detective with the Queensland Police Force and his colleague, David Morris, an equally experienced journalist, have collaborated to provide our society and, importantly, families and young people, with a graphic insight into the world of the internet sexual predator. This is not just an issue impacting on other parts of the world; indeed, we here in Australia are seeing the increasing phenomenon that is internet-based sexual predatory behaviour, and one that is clearly focused on seeking out the most vulnerable members of our community — our children and our teenagers.

Through using case studies and analysis, Brett and

David take us into the world that, thankfully, many of us do not know, namely, that of the internet sexual predator. The authors seek to develop our knowledge of the predator who, for the most part, is unseen and unknown, and the predator whose background, skills, and qualifications are varied and not stereotyped, and whose predilections are complex and confused.

The tools of trade of these predators involve one of the greatest information boons of our time, namely, the internet. It is a wonderful tool that educates, informs, and provides almost limitless insights into things historic and contemporary, and allows us to peek into the future. Whilst it provides immediate access into a rich array of information, like many things in life, it provides an avenue for those who would misuse this technology to engage in inappropriate conduct and behaviour. Indeed, the use of the internet for sexual misconduct or gratification is but one example of its misuse.

The victims of such predacious behaviour are not limited to a single gender, age group, or culture. The growing nature of the problem is a worldwide one, and whilst governments mandate to control such behaviour (with all their predictable slowness to respond), one critical tool remains at our immediate disposal — parenting. The authors complement their case studies and commentary with suggestions of how parents can exercise a number of sensible controls. These controls have to be based in trust in our children, effective communication with our children, support for our

children, and, importantly, the ongoing education of our children. We owe our children that much.

We read of the five stages of predatory behaviour and the motivations of those who engage in such conduct. As parents, grandparents, and family members, the authors seek to develop in us an understanding of those who engage in sexual predatory behaviour and how, through vigilance and support, we can protect our greatest asset — our children.

The authors take us into the world of the undercover police operative where men and women working in one of the most challenging areas of policing are focused at local, national, and international levels on addressing the issue. We owe these officers a great deal of gratitude for what they do for, and on, our behalf. This work imposes a responsibility on Police Force Command to develop and deliver ongoing education and training, counselling and welfare programs for police officers in order to ensure they too do not become unintended or secondary victims of this criminal conduct.

I commend Brett and David for their work and trust the reader will find it informative and enhance their understanding of the critical role that we can play (alongside law enforcement) in addressing and combatting this behaviour.

K. E. MORONEY AO APM
NSW Commissioner of Police (Retired)

1
Smoke and Mirrors
— Detective Work Online

As a former police officer of twenty-two years and undercover internet detective, as well as a father, I am uniquely qualified and passionate about informing parents of the online risks to their children. I've arrested over a thousand people for criminal offences. For most of my sixteen years as a detective, I investigated adult people who were looking to seriously harm or abuse children.

For five years, it was my job to go undercover on the internet, pretending to be a young person. I spent thousands of hours using chat rooms, messaging programs, and online games such as WOW, Cod, Runescape, Mushy Monsters, Club Penguin, and Minecraft. As a 'teenager', I've frequented dozens of social networking sites such as Facebook, My Space, Speed Boat, Tag, Twitter, and Flicker. I know how these programs work inside and out, so I have a clear perspective on what it means to be a young person online, how young people communicate with each other, and how adults with wrong intentions communicate with me. I personally arrested eighty-nine adults for their activity on these sites.

I also had the opportunity to work with the US

Department of Homeland Security at its cybercrimes centre in Virginia, US, the FBI undercover internet team, and the Dallas and San Jose Police Internet Crimes Against Children Task Forces. I left the police to work for the US Government in Iraq, training Iraqi men to be police officers. I now speak to young people and families about safeguarding their loved ones online. I have a unique connection with young people, in that I was one of them on the internet.

Prior to going online and undercover for the Queensland Crime and Misconduct Commission in 2002, I thought I had seen it all as a police officer. I had investigated everything from shop theft through to murder. Nothing could shock me anymore, could it? My first time on gaming and social networking sites turned this perception on its head. I was shocked at how many conversations were occurring simultaneously and how aggressively people talked to each other. It seemed as though everyone online had a false sense of confidence. They were sharing or saying things they wouldn't dare share or say in person. It felt as though verbal bullets were whizzing all around. Communication on the internet seemed like the Wild West — little structure or etiquette, and a pervading feeling of lawlessness.

My assignment as an undercover officer appeared simple: enter the internet world, engage with suspicious people attempting to commit a crime, and build a portfolio of evidence substantial enough to ensure the laws could charge and convict them. Frequenting

young people's social networking, gaming, and communication sites and programs, one minute I pretended to be a fourteen year old boy, and the next a thirteen year old girl — I suspect I have been a teenage girl on the internet longer than nearly any teenage girl in Australia's history. Tracking down predators who roam the internet seeking to satisfy evil desires at the expense of destroying young lives, then seeing them convicted, was a satisfying contribution to the wider effort required to protect the young online.

Internet policing was in its pioneer stage when I started. Concealed behind a computer screen, I learnt how predators think and operate. I also experienced how a child would feel, as the predator doesn't hold back when he thinks he is talking to a potential victim. Despite policing child exploitation before going online, I was shocked by the uninhibited nature of the conversations.

The role of an undercover police detective could be likened to method acting, where the actor becomes fully immersed in the part they are playing in order to be convincing. Detectives step into the shoes of different fictitious teenagers to engage with threatening characters in scenarios where the stakes are high and people's lives can be irreversibly affected. With the predator as the audience they are trying to convince, they need to pull off their detective work flawlessly. Anonymity gives them the time in a controlled environment to practise and perfect their roles. To gather enough evidence to apprehend these people, a

detective's performance needs to be totally consistent and believable.

In the course of this work, detectives view child abuse messages, pictures, and videos. They communicate online with people suspected of being involved in child grooming offences — that is, stalkers seeking to desensitise young minds by exposing them to increasingly explicit sexual information and images. While tracking these offenders, detectives communicate with hundreds of people online who are doing the right thing. Weeding out the bad guys, sometimes involves infiltrating predator online communities by assuming the identities of fictitious paedophiles to learn how their kind think, network, interact, and behave. It involves text-based conversations and exchanging images and videos, including webcam.

Some detectives are able to treat the activity as a job, passing off what they encounter as simply 'dealing with data', but this is not the case for all. The investigator's experience of becoming immersed in charades of this nature can weigh heavily. Online police experience the full brunt of the hostility of predators who think they are dealing with vulnerable teenagers.

The effect of online intimidation on young people's minds has been widely publicised. Bombarding children with indecent pictures and videos is bullying at its most extreme. As well as written abuse, children are subjected to indecent and illegal materials as the predator tries to desensitise them and draw them into their web. Similarly, during their investigations,

detectives are confronted with obscene posts and vast amounts of other disturbing material. They deal with countless images and footage of children being abused.

Offenders arrested for attempting to lure a child online usually have vast collections of child exploitation material, which in layman's terms is simply child pornography, depicting the basest acts. Examining this disturbing material can have a deep effect.

Using a computer mouse to click in and out of games and communication sites, I held random conversations with strangers and quickly learnt to identify adults who shouldn't be there. I was sickened by how these people with criminal intentions approached young people. They had unrestricted access to young lives in a way that was not possible before the dawn of the internet. They were committing serious offences by making very deliberate approaches to children, unaware that they were really communicating with police officers who were busily recording their actions. I learnt to record programs and capture evidence, copying and pasting it from online conversations onto a running sheet.

Legal systems have had to continue to adapt to address the spread of crime online. In my home state since 2000, many significant changes have been made to the way the criminal justice system has prevented and responded to incidents of online child sexual victimisation. These changes in the law have allowed detectives to go online to track down perpetrators. Adding Section 218A to the Queensland Criminal Code

in 2003 was ground breaking in Australia. The new law enabled more proactive prosecution of predators using the internet to target children under sixteen.

Section 218A made it an offence for adults to use electronic communication with the intent of procuring a child or a person the adult believes is under sixteen years of age to engage in a sexual act. The most powerful word in that legislation, enforcement wise, is 'believe'. The section makes it easier for police to secure a conviction, not only for physical violence but also based on the accused's 'intent'. This means police do not have to show the child exists, or that there is a real child, only that the offender 'believed' as much. This enables police to assume fictitious teen identities, and for these assumed identities to form the basis of the offence. No real child needs to be involved.

Online detectives become proficient at communicating, gathering evidence, piecing it all together, and storing it in the right place. The approach is different from all other forms of investigation in the physical world. By visiting online spaces where young people meet and relate to others their age, a detective does not have to look far for predators. Predators find them.

It is not difficult for a detective to become believable as a twelve year old girl. They can simply Google or ask other users questions, and observe how young girls act and the photos and programs they use. Swinging into action as their child alias gives them an opportunity that not many have: to view the internet from a completely

different perspective. While imitating a child online, the detective looks at technology as a child would, viewing it through the eyes of an adult detective pretending to be a child. They look for signals young people would not pick up. They develop incredible insights into human nature from the multiple perspectives of a child, teen, adult, and predator. They learn what predatory behaviour looks like, and begin to predict the next question, comment, or action of the predator.

Predators have questions they need to ask, and answers and information they require as they move towards satisfying their illegal objectives. Police investigative methodology is precise and picks up the predator's veiled intentions. Online investigations have been a huge success, resulting in hundreds of people being arrested.

2
Trusting Your Gut Instinct

The experiences of an online detective led me to ask, 'Why are children, and even adults, fooled online by people with wrong intentions?' Victims of online abuse do not come from a single socio-economic group. Many are highly intelligent.

Answers came as I continued communicating with online offenders and gathering evidence. I learnt that predators use the same methods to entice potential victims as those I investigated in the physical world. They are just more candid when they think no authority figure is present to shelter their intended victim.

Predators are potentially present in all young people's forums, including games, social networks, chat and communication programs and websites. As an online officer, I learnt how to identify them quickly. The key is to pick up the predator's intentions early, then gather evidence leading to their arrest and prosecution.

I learnt the way to address child exploitation online is the same as in the physical world. It involves common sense, trusting the instinct that tells you something is not quite right. Where I come from, this is called 'smelling a rat'. It is this protective instinct that causes parents to take precautions when someone hangs around a park where their child is playing. They watch

for anything suspicious, step in where needed, and teach their child to be careful. These similarities lead to the simple premise of this book, demystifying for parents the task of safeguarding their children online:

As both the physical and cyber worlds are the meeting places of humans, and human nature in all its facets has not really changed, how we deal with issues online should be no different to how we deal with them in the physical world.

That being noted, I discovered something disturbingly different in the online playground — the widespread lack of parental supervision, even in close-knit families. Parents would never leave their children isolated and at risk if they knew the level of danger that faced their child. Many mums and dads see their child pre-occupied on a computer as a chance to have a break. 'They're quiet, so that's a good thing' is a common attitude; or 'I don't want to disturb them because that only makes them irritable.' However, parenting should not be turned off when the computer is turned on. The internet provides a wonderful forum for children to explore possibilities and learn about the physical world, but while it is full of enriching experiences, it is necessary for parents to keep watch as their child learns about life in 'the playground'.

By 'children' I refer to all age groups that adults are legally responsible for, from primary school age to teenagers. A son might be taller than his parent and

have facial hair, or a daughter might be fully developed and want her total independence, but they do not yet have life skills that parents, grandparents, teachers, and other mature role models have learnt from experience. By applying shared community values and common sense, boundaries put in place will protect children online and enable them to enjoy interacting on the internet in a safe and positive manner.

While the internet continues to grow and provide exciting educational and communication opportunities for young people, I have seen the dark side. I have spoken to predators and asked them how they pick their targets. They relentlessly seek out young people who show by their online actions that they are susceptible. They look for teenagers who oversexualise behaviours or portray themselves as someone else. Those with dishonest motives see this as a sure indicator of low self-esteem and vulnerability.

Increasingly mobile technology in the form of smart phones requires decisive parenting. Portable devices make it easier for young people to conduct online activity away from supervision, thus increasing the risk of being targeted by predators. Children at increasingly younger ages are watching adult material as new technology sneaks pornography into their pockets. Their innocence is their online Achilles' heel.

When I began online investigations in 2002, internet detective work was new in Australia. Since then, internet usage has escalated and children are more

involved in the online community at a younger age. When I began speaking on internet safety in 2008, ninety per cent of schools and colleges I visited were secondary and ten per cent were primary. Now it is '50-50'. I speak at schools where children in Year 2 are issued their own iPads with internet access. Their chances of being exposed to dubious internet content early rises significantly.

The scenarios detailed in the following pages occur online daily. Unlawful use of technology is an issue that will not disappear. However, we as a community, parents, carers, educators, and law enforcement can reduce the risks for our young people.

By pretending to be a child online, I have seen through a child's eyes why adults must intervene on their behalf. My advice is based on first-hand accounts of what children and young people encounter without parents knowing.

Parents, I hope to open your eyes and spark a passion in you to get involved and the self-belief that you have the instincts and life skills your child needs to learn in the online environment. As you read, I hope it becomes clear to you how important your role is and that:

> *What you can do, is exactly what you do in the physical world — you can educate your child to identify and avoid dangers, teach them how to deal with these dangers, and put strategies in place to significantly reduce the risk of negative outcomes online.*

3
Feeling Bullied and Intimidated

A change in a child's behaviour after time on the computer can usually be traced to their interactions with other online users. Most predators use bullying and intimidation when they establish contact with a child, or at some stage during grooming and offending; although they are not the only ones who treat children aggressively. Children can often be cruel to each other. Parents would do well to realise that when their child experiences issues on the internet and seems to change, it generally has nothing to do with technology; it has to do with how people are treating them.

The internet can be a very lonely place where victims of bullying feel worthless and alone. It affects them mentally. There is nothing tangible they can grasp. It feels like the most isolated place that a person will ever find themselves. The words communicated to them go straight into their minds and build wrong and dangerous perceptions. For those already struggling with negative self-esteem, being fed this type of perception twenty-four/seven can be very damaging. The enemy they do not know feeding them this rubbish is always worse than the one they do know.

The online detective experiences these feelings too and needs to learn to deal with them. Communicating

with fellow officers about their negative emotions helps. The best advice for those experiencing online intimidation, and for parents whose children who are being affected by something they cannot put their finger on, is to Communicate! Transparent communication with trusted friends and family is the most basic, yet powerful, weapon to address online issues.

After several months of online investigating, I grew increasingly angry, frustrated, and intimidated. I experienced firsthand what a young person, or anyone for that matter, feels when they are cyber bullied. As I could not express online how it was affecting me, I transferred the way I felt into the physical world and expressed it in real-life situations. I took it out on my workmates and family. Eventually, when I aired my frustrations by sending an angry email to a colleague, I realised that my growing aggression stemmed from my internet encounters. The negative content I was being subjected to was changing me as a person. The experience helped me to understand how young people and adults can be pushed to the edge. From then on, I was required to see a psychologist every six months. Each working shift, I took a mandatory break after two hours online to walk down the street and have a chat with real people. I was never allowed to work on my own. It made a real difference having that support and feeling I was not isolated from the physical world.

If negative online communication impacts seasoned police officers, who see more than most in the physical

world, consider the effect it can have on the young and impressionable. This is why children should be deterred from hiding themselves away in their bedrooms or a closed study on their computers. Instead, good habits and positive mindsets towards technology can be nurtured in their lives, especially from a young age. Educating children about the online world will protect them. The more parents are involved in guiding online usage, the safer children will be.

Some parents still have limited understanding of the online realities their children face. While this ignorance is likely to diminish within another generation online, many parents were never taught the effect online intrusions by strangers can have on a young mind staring continuously at a computer.

The first step in dealing with online manipulation is simple — identify how the whole experience is affecting the victim. It can even have an effect without them knowing. Helping them to acknowledge what is happening creates an opportunity to deal with it.

The same approach can help people who suffer with self-esteem issues. Firstly, acknowledge what is causing the distress and secondly, talk about it with trusted people in the physical world. The issue can then be addressed more rationally. It is important for them to recognise that the negative messages received do not reflect on them as a person.

Too many victims have not known where to turn and, as a result, have taken their own lives. Others and their families have been deeply, and at times, irreversibly,

scarred. People who do not have the courage to say face to face the hurtful and deeply impacting comments they post, often perpetrate the bullying. Anyone of any age subjected to this type of intimidation has a right to do something about it.

The first time I shared with a person in the physical world my anguish over the buffeting I was getting online, it demystified the experience for me and I found that my ability to deal with the ongoing negativity improved one hundred fold.

While vigilance by parents may head off much of the aggressive treatment of their children, most children will be subjected to online intimidation at some stage in their formative years. The cumulative effect of online pressure on a child, by either a predator or an immature, vindictive or mischievous peer, can be impossible for them to deal with on their own. However, that doesn't mean it cannot be dealt with very effectively with support.

4
Steps to Minimise the Impacts

I t is important for children and adults to know they can be charged for cyber bullying.

While legislation might not mention the words, many criminal offences in Australia are a good fit for cyber bullying. One is a federal offence involving 'any person using a carriage service to menace, harass or threaten.' It is very clear. Adults and children over the age of criminal responsibility are frequently being charged for cyber bullying under this legislation. It is important to know the exact wording of this offence. Who can be subject to this legislation? The offence does not say 'an adult person', 'a person who is not a student', or 'everybody except me' — it says 'any person'.

Knowing that online bullying is a serious community issue gives hope to anyone who is ever on the receiving end and enables them to work effectively through it. No one should feel they are left to helplessly endure online harassment. Something can be done about it. Whether or not a parent believes legal advice needs to be sourced, their child should be taught their rights and responsibilities in dealing with others online.

As in Australia, many jurisdictions around the world now have legislation prohibiting online bullying, classifying it as a criminal offence. Of the countless

cases of cyber bullying raised by students, their schools, and parents, most can be resolved quickly and effortlessly, or at least to the victim's satisfaction.

Solutions generally begin with a conversation in the physical world. When primary school children are asked what they do when they have a problem or feel unsafe in the physical world, they nearly always answer, 'I speak with a trusted adult.' That is how they are conditioned. They are taught who can help and protect them.

Sadly, unless they are educated, children who are being bullied normally keep quiet about it. Reasons may include:

- Fear of losing technology

- Embarrassment

- Feeling that it is their fault

- Thinking that it is just what happens online

- Believing that nothing can be done.

A child's online behaviours and attitudes can be moulded positively — just as they are in the physical world. From the day, they begin their internet journey, they should be instructed, 'I do not just encourage you to speak to me if you have a problem online, I expect you to speak to me.' Further, 'I will not remove your technology.

We can talk, and I will help you solve the problem so you can get on with having a good time on the internet.'

While speaking to a group of schoolgirls, I asked, 'Why do people cyber bully others?' I did not expect well-thought-out answers, but found it interesting that every response recognised the act says more about the bully than their victim:

'They are angry about something, and they are taking it out on others.'

'They are jealous of the other person.'

'They are being bullied themselves and think it will make them feel better.'

'They are scared it might happen to them, so they do it to feel safe.'

'Maybe their friends are doing it, and they feel pressured.'

'They don't like who they are and want to feel powerful.'

The girls recognised that the cyber bullying has nothing to do with the victim. Not one child answered, 'What they are saying is the truth' or, 'The victim is ugly, or weird, or unpopular.' The girls' astute insight is a real key to deflecting the psychological impacts of bullying. They are acknowledging that if someone bullies them, 'It is not about me. Rather, it is about them.'

A teacher asked eleven year old students to write down points they had learnt during one of my presentations. One student wrote, 'If someone is nasty to me on the internet, it means that they think I am better than them.' Parents need to have these discussions

with their children. These discussions need to be ongoing and reinforced by parents' actions.

Learning to choose online friends carefully is essential not only for children but also for parents. A parent told me they received a friend request from a neighbour through Facebook. They generally only associated in a neighbourly fashion by waving as they passed in the street. Without thinking, they accepted the neighbour's friend request and came to regret making the connection. They became concerned with the messages and language the neighbour used. They learned he was not someone their family would associate with in person. However, the parent did not want to block or unfriend the neighbour, because he might not appreciate it and cause issues in the street. This is an example of a person's online decisions being controlled by someone else.

Many children feel threatened by other users when they visit certain sites and use particular programs. The obvious answer, an adult would conclude is 'Get out of the program.' Children need to be taught to feel free to choose to opt out. They can be trained to be confident in making this choice. Why would they stay there? Nobody wants to feel uncomfortable, threatened, or bad about themselves. Why stay somewhere when they feel like that? Children generally do not stay in the firing line in the physical world; they should know it is not normal to remain exposed to poor treatment in the cyber world either. This is a critical skill to learn that will help a child dismiss a predator's approaches early on.

If children are being bullied or harassed online, it is a good idea to save a copy of the offending information. One of the best parts of the detective's job investigating and dealing with child sex offenders is when the culprit is sitting in the interview room being questioned after their arrest. They give many excuses, thinking they can talk their way out of the allegations. Some initially deny they have used a chat program, and stress they never did anything indecent. Some even accuse the child of being the aggressor, talking crudely and sending inappropriate material. Some claim they are trying to help and protect the child online 'because there are bad men out there.' At this point, it is satisfying to push a tall pile of paper across the desk detailing every conversation, connection, interaction, image, and dealing the detective has had with them while acting undercover. The record includes dates and times down to the second. After reading one or maybe two pages, the predator's usual reaction is to look up from the page and say, 'Well, yep, it looks like you got me.'

Keeping a record of online interactions needn't be just to supply evidence to police. The evidence can be used to ensure conversations are based on facts, not perceptions or misinterpretations of the truth. Schools rely on students and parents to provide evidence of cyber bullying before they begin discussions with all participants in the chat. It can help parents support their children to solve their problems quickly and get on with having a good time online.

Steps to minimise the impacts of bullying:

- Communicate
- Understand bullying is about the bully, not the victim
- Document evidence.

5
Realising It Is a
Very Public Internet

An English couple flew into the US on holiday. Upon arrival, they were startled when Customs enforcement escorted them to a room to be interviewed by the Department of Homeland Security. Homeland Security advised them that a software scan detected the man had used the word 'destroy' in a tweet. He had a difficult time explaining that he was only joking to friends before leaving for the US when he tweeted, 'I just want to have one last drink with you guys before I go and destroy America.' His girlfriend was also implicated because he tweeted that she was a big Marilyn Monroe fan and that he might dig up the deceased movie star for her. A search for shovels in their suitcases followed, with the Englishman regretting ever making the tweets.

Because America places enormous value in online surveillance to identify mindsets and intentions of concern and head off threatening behaviours, this couple was subsequently deported.

Having seen the worst the internet holds for children, I am convinced that mentoring the young in its usage is far more effective in safeguarding them than barring them from using it. Parents would be ill advised to put

a rule in place that says 'No' to technology. Children should not miss out. However, their futures are safeguarded when home internet usage controls are put in place. A key reason for this is that most children are unaware everything they post is widely accessible. Even with privacy settings in place, it only takes one 'friend' to forward on a post and it is in the public domain.

It surprises young people when they learn that their online identity is public. That is why they are prepared to have a discussion with a stranger on the internet without giving it any thought. They believe the conversation is private and there is no way the person on the other end will ever learn their true identity or physical location.

Before visiting a high school to speak to students, teachers, and parents about internet safety, I search for social network accounts of students attending that school. I place sourced photographs of students up on the big screen for the whole school to see. I would never deliberately post a photo that leaves a student open to ridicule, but I do make sure they are thinking about what is really going on here. It usually shocks them when a photo copied from their site is shown. A common reaction is, 'Hey, that's private!' To which I reply, 'Well, it is on the screen, and everyone is looking at it, so it is not private.'

Regardless of whether young people think their posts are private, the fact is what they put online is not secure. It is better that students consider this now than later when the false belief causes an issue in their life.

Young people say and believe each of their online posts is private; they may even demand it remains private, but that does always not mean it does. They are shocked to learn their images can be accessed without any special software, even when privacy settings have been put in place. While use of privacy settings should be encouraged, no online program can guarantee total privacy. Young people trust the people they have shared the image with will respect their privacy, but time and again captured images are on-forwarded. Similarly, they expect their information will remain secure on social networking sites, yet internet companies continually redefine privacy settings and who information is shared with.

Young people are sobered by this thought when it is shown to them in a classroom setting. When they are told, 'If you control your information on the internet, I would not have it, but I have got it,' the mood in the room changes. At this revelation, students look at each other, look down, look up, or have a confused or shocked look on their faces. This indicates they are confronted with a truth they have never considered before. They are under a very dangerous misconception. They think their internet experience finishes when they walk away from their computer.

This misconception needs to be addressed.

A greater understanding of the nature of the internet will enable them to make informed online choices.

A classroom exercise with male students aged fourteen to sixteen never fails to get the point across

when I begin by saying, 'I often visit young people's social networking profiles and see a certain "style" of photograph that is very common among boys around your age. It is not a particular photo, it is a style of photo.'

The students look puzzled and some grow concerned. 'Yeah, you know the ones. You are standing in front of the mirror in your bathroom.'

A change sets in in the audience. Some nod, while others shift in their seats. '...and you've got the door closed because you do not want your parents to see. That could be embarrassing.'

Cut the atmosphere with a knife! The class cannot sit still. Some boys laugh, mostly nervously.

'You have got your phone. You point it at the mirror. You lift your shirt and you take a photo...of your abs.'

Pandemonium sets in. Red and white-faced friends share looks and laughter. Others plant their faces in their hands.

'Yeah, guys, and then in a split second you press upload and that photo goes straight to your social networking site for your closest three billion friends to see. You do it to impress the ladies. I get it. But think about this — the principal is in their office right now looking at that photo on a computer, or your grandma is in the retirement village logging in to a computer to show her friends a photo of her grandson. She and her friends are looking at that photo right now.' Judging by students' expressions, this is not something they had considered. While I do not show compromising photos

to the class when conducting this exercise, to use the boys' words, they feel 'icky'.

Most users think social media companies provide the site for them simply so they can enjoy chatting with friends, but this is only a part of the picture. Social media is provided for free to *gather information about users for marketing purposes.* Every word on a Facebook page is strategically positioned. The user cannot alter the basic format. That is because it is designed to capture user information and pass it on to advertisers to target the individual. While social media companies seek to be responsible by providing privacy safeguards to protect children, their programs are all about gathering information to sell! Google makes no secret about this fact, proclaiming, 'We are a digital information vacuum cleaner.'

All popular programs on the internet exist for this same reason — to make money. This does not make them intrinsically bad, but users should be aware of how they operate. If users are not discrete, the information sites share is accessible to people they normally would not want to view it. If you are not paying for content on the internet, *you are the content.*

A site's popularity is determined by successful marketing. Mention 'Instagram' to young people and they get excited. They love it and not because the program is brilliant. It is because Instagram has marketed itself well to children.

Children do not use Facebook because they choose

to. They are being 'told' to use Facebook. They did not review every social networking site on the internet and say, 'Well, that is the best one for me.' They use Facebook because 'everyone else does.' Not long ago all Australian teenagers used Myspace, and Facebook was 'for old people.' While trends change, the purpose does not. Facebook and Instagram are all about information flowing and connecting people. Often that is good, sometimes it is bad. Every time children log on, they are connected to strangers. Because those people are unseen, it is particularly hard for a young person to conceptualise how public a forum it really is. Children need to be taught.

Privacy on the internet is not based on fact; it is an illusion based on people's own expectations. No one has privacy or control over their information after they upload or send it. That becomes someone else's decision. When the public nature of the internet is demonstrated in a personal way to young people, their mindsets are forced to change. Feelings of privacy, control, anonymity, and believing that they are in a different world to the physical world, are dangerously false. It is a mindset that needs to change.

If you are not paying for content online, You Are the Content. There is no 'real' privacy on the internet.

6
The Law Still Applies

At times, police are accused of being unethical by pretending to be underage children online. However, detectives engage in these types of investigations to identify and remove dangerous people from society online, just as they do in the physical world.

Opinion is also divided on whether the public should be alerted to the levels of policing presence online. Those opposed, argue that it will alert potential criminals; those for, maintain that awareness will act as a deterrent. Society — including predators — is now fully aware there is policing activity online. Whether anyone agrees or not, the knowledge is out there.

The police detective's role is not to induce a predator to commit a criminal offence, which is often frowned upon by courts. However, just as children have a right to be active online, so do police. It is important for policing to occur in both the cyber and physical worlds because both are the real world. It is also important for potential online offenders to understand that law enforcers have a presence online. This will not deter all of them, but it does keep them guessing how, when, and where police might apprehend them. Therefore, the detective turns up to work in corporate attire — wearing a business shirt, dress pants, and a tie, and plays games with other

members of the online community. They know if they visit a stockbroking website, they are unlikely to identify child predators because children do not go there. They make no apology for frequenting the sites where children go and pretending to be one of them. Detectives spend thousands of hours communicating with children and adults on the internet with the intention to protect the young and innocent.

When asked if I needed counselling after hours of undercover duties online, I replied, 'Yes, but not only because I had to talk to paedophiles all day, it is also because I had to talk about Hannah Montana all day!'

The police detective's motive for interacting with child sex offenders online is to gather evidence to prove their guilt. The evidence needs to stand up in a court of law. Detectives know full well that people's legal responsibility to abide by the law is as real online as in the physical world. Yet many apprehended predators think that what they are doing isn't so bad — even though they are soliciting children.

Predators try to minimise the seriousness of online activity, saying 'it is only words and pictures.' However, that mindset is false and based on ignorance. Downplaying the seriousness of posting and sharing online child exploitation materials does not stand up as a defence in court. When offenders are jailed for their illegal online behaviour, they are not sentenced to 'cyber prison' — there is no such place. They have committed real crimes and go to a real prison.

Detectives' methods of recording screen activity

for evidence are rapidly becoming more sophisticated. When online detective work first began, police made a real-time screen recording using a large video camera set on a tripod directly behind where they were sitting. A huge lens literally rested on their shoulders, directed at the screen. This was always present and was a physical world reminder there would always be a copy of every key the detective typed, every choice they made. For detectives, it could not be denied that while they were communicating through a screen, they were operating in and would be judged in the physical world.

The undercover detective makes decisions based on the knowledge that their interaction will be rigorously scrutinised when they sit in a witness box in front of a judge and jury. They must always consider and imagine this when making choices, asking or answering questions, or posting information. Everything the detective does is being recorded, forcing them to condition themselves to the internet environment. It gives them a very clear understanding of the nature of the internet. It highlights the seriousness of online choices and perceived privacy and anonymity issues for all internet users. This awareness is not instinctive and must be learned.

Many adults are making mistakes while learning about the online experience. Some think they would never hurt a child in person and that they are simply expressing their thoughts and dark desires on the internet in a digital form. They find it difficult to conceive they are carrying out their fantasies with a real child and affecting that child as much as if they were

abusing them in person. Even those who intentionally use the internet to victimise and harm children are deceived into thinking what they are doing is harmless, until it leads into the physical world. Adults committing online offences range from the naïve and curious to the evil, but they all should know that what they are doing is illegal and subject to prosecution.

There is no all-encompassing profile of individuals looking for or prepared to harm a child. Desires and methods vary. Psychologically, they are chipping away at that child's innocence, desensitising them for their own gratification and self-satisfaction. While some might not harm a child in person, they are having the same effect online and need to be held accountable.

Before the internet, most crimes committed against children were by people the victim knew. However, the growth of the internet has led to a dramatic increase in crimes committed by offenders not known to the victim, at least not in the physical world. These extra-familial predators have gained access to victims they would not have been able to target without the internet.

A dramatic spike in networked and organised paedophilia has accompanied the internet's growth. Online, predators prey on children in neighbourhoods near and far, identify the most vulnerable, and groom them for sexual abuse. Geographical boundaries do not come into play. Children without parental supervision — like sheep who have strayed from a shepherd's flock — are more of a target.

Predators now have greater access and falsely believe they can stay anonymous and beyond the arm of the law, making them less inhibited about offending against children online. Many of them find it easier to offend by showing children pornography or pornographic acts on the screen because they can de-personalise a child they cannot physically see. While the child they are offending against by sharing inappropriate material is a real, flesh and blood person, the offender reduces that child to data on a screen. They do not need to view them as a real person.

While targeting and arresting predators, police come across many children who are doing the wrong thing. No one ever imagines it is going to be them sitting in the principal's office, boss's office or police station justifying the choices they make online. By typing the wrong key in the privacy of their home or pushing the wrong button on their phone as they walk down the street, they are unwittingly committing criminal offences they could be prosecuted for. Crimes that are facilitated by technology are treated no differently by the judicial system to crimes committed face to face.

Most offences that police charge users with, for making the wrong choices online, have to do with the impacts on people and property, and their arrests are based on community expectations. Most are also for committing the same offences online that existed before the internet was ever conceived.

Let's say David wants to sell a guitar and uses the

online shopping program eBay to advertise the sale. He posts a photograph of his guitar on eBay and people bid on it. The highest bidder buys the guitar and transfers money into David's bank account. But guess what? David does not have a guitar. He was short on cash that week, so he sourced a photo of a guitar from Google Images and posted it on eBay.

People bid on a non-existent item, and someone bought it when he had no intent at any stage of supplying the product. David has committed a criminal offence.

If the guitar buyer made a complaint to police, David would be arrested for fraud. He received the money knowing he could not supply the advertised product.

Now, say David was standing in front of the judge. The judge would read out the charge to him, and the prosecution would be required to prove that charge. The charge would read, 'That on a specified date at a specified place, David lawfully defrauded one "John Smith" of a sum of money, namely $150.' The charge makes no mention of technology, eBay, or the internet. What David has done has had nothing to do with technology. He has defrauded another human being. The charge is the same as if he had committed the offence in person or before the internet was invented.

Children can commit online crimes without even realising it. Currently in Australia, a child can be arrested for forwarding a naked photo of themselves to other children. The parents of the other child might complain, and the culprit is arrested. Committing the act online makes it no less serious than similar actions

in person. This devastating consequence can happen to any young person who makes a wrong choice. It is assumed every young person knows right from wrong, and they have no reason to ignore how they transfer those beliefs into how they use technology. Even online they are dealing with real people.

The law assumes internet users know their responsibilities online, and that the nature of that world is no different from the physical world. It is about communicating with real people, so laws, rules, responsibilities, and rights have not changed. Children must be taught that their rights do not increase when they get behind a screen and others' rights do not decrease either. Every good choice helps when it comes to technology.

Is the internet ever going to be a perfect place? No. Are predators and cyber bullies ever going to be eradicated? No. What we can do, though, is exactly what we do in the physical world — educate children to identify and avoid dangers, teach them how to deal with these dangers, and put strategies in place to reduce the risk of negative outcomes.

There are real world consequences for virtual reality crimes.

7
You Have the Right
to Remain Silent!

Freedom of speech is something many communities have the privilege of living under, yet I wonder what our forefathers would have thought if they knew where it has led today.

Exercising the right to free speech seems straightforward and self-explanatory; however, this is not entirely the case when it is put to the test. Just because people can say what they want does not mean there will not be, or should not be, a consequence. Freedom of speech does not and never was intended to mean a person can say whatever they want, whenever they want, to whomever they want. Parents already know this, and so do their children.

If a student walks into the principal's office and yells abuse, threatens, and swears, the principal would not sit there and say, 'Well, there is nothing I can do because you have freedom of speech.' Everyone knows the response would be far different. The student's future at that school may be in jeopardy.

Other common examples in society where a person's speech is readily called to account are defamation and racial vilification. Most people have that inbuilt gauge to know most times what is and is not appropriate. Why

can that gauge be trusted? Because there are rewards for avoiding the penalties. If the student in the example trusts what he knows when considering what he says to the principal, he will avoid being penalised.

Most people are instinctively smart enough to stick to saying what is appropriate, particularly when they have the aid of social indicators in the physical world. Parents can instil this mindset in their children so that they can rightly gauge their online choices. By making choices based on a more considered thought process, they will only say something they are prepared to say in person and will reap the same reward by avoiding issues.

Being accountable for what we say in public is a good thing. If these verbal boundaries were not there, others could say and treat children however they wanted without recourse, because 'They have freedom of speech.' That is a world we do not want to live in. We cannot just say whatever we like. As an online police detective, when predators made inappropriate comments to me believing they were communicating with a teen, they were arrested and charged for those conversations. The words they used to the person they believed they were talking to constituted a criminal offence and led to jail time.

In early 2014, an Australian court ordered a defendant who posted defamatory statements on Twitter and Facebook about a schoolteacher to pay $105,000 in compensatory damages. The decision, the first of its kind in Australia, indicates the legal system will not tolerate personal attacks using social media. The court

heard the defendant held a grudge against the teacher, believing she had something to do with his father, also a teacher, leaving the school. The court ruled there was no evidence to substantiate the belief. The complainant had an established and excellent reputation and many years' experience, and taught in the school's music and arts department. The defendant was an ex-student of the school and son of a former music and arts teacher who left the school in 2008 to attend to personal issues. After the defendant was warned on social media to be careful what he posted online, he replied, 'I can post whatever the "f-" I like. I don't give a shit…if anyone gets hurt over what I have to say about her.'

The judge accepted that the effect of the publications on the complainant was 'devastating'. The teacher immediately took sick leave and at the time of the hearings was only returning to work on a limited basis. The complainant told the court that if it weren't for the defamatory publications, she would have continued to teach for a further seven years until she reached sixty-five. The judge said the award of damages in defamation cases was intended to vindicate the person's reputation in the eyes of the general community and compensate her for the distress and insult felt.

The judge ordered the defendant to pay $85,000 in compensatory damages and a further $20,000 in aggravated damages. Aggravated damages were awarded because the defendant ignored a letter from the teacher's lawyers, only removing the comments and apologising after they wrote to him a second time,

and because he amended his defence to argue that the comments posted were true, which was held to contradict the sincerity of his apology.

The judge said in his judgment: 'When defamatory publications are made on social media, it is common knowledge that they spread. They spread easily by the simple manipulation of mobile phones and computers. Their evil lies in the grapevine effect that stems from the use of this type of communication. I have taken that into account in the assessment of damages that I previously made.'

The laws in Australia also enable anyone who forwards on or repeats a defamatory statement to be sued for defamation. Retweeting defamatory material can also land children in hot water.

The complainant's lawyer said the judgment 'drew a line in the sand for those who up until now have used social media to defame others, to hurt them and think there are no consequences. If someone wants to continue to do it despite being warned, it is particularly appalling, as it was in this case.'

The case highlights that the principles of defamation law apply equally to statements made on social media as to publication in other forms of media.

Children will not naturally keep legal issues such as defamation in the front of their mind while social networking. Social media may be instantaneous, but it is not as short lived as a victim of online intimidation might hope. The Australian court case illustrates that online actions can have a lasting physical life impact.

Social media posts can be subject to defamation. Parents must teach their children not only to think before they speak, but also to think before they post anything online.

Freedom of speech does not permit defamation of others to occur.

8
Make the Virtual World Real

Teaching children 'stranger danger' is one of the most important ways parents safeguard their children in the physical world. Despite this, strangers are winning the confidence of children online — right under their parents' noses. There is no doubting how every mum and dad would react if their son turned up at home, saying, 'I have made a new friend. He is new to our neighbourhood. He loves playing the same games as me and he listens to everything I have to say. He is thirty-two years old. If you don't mind, Mum and Dad, my new friend and I are going to play on the internet in my bedroom?' Yet each day and night our children are engaging and interacting with adults over the internet. Everyone's gut instinct says this is wrong but as adults and parents, we often are blissfully unaware that this is happening, or even how simple it is for us to prevent.

Parents teaching children 'stranger danger' and then leaving them largely unsupervised is not enough to fully protect them in either the cyber or the physical world. I conclusively demonstrated this with the support of four families on the national Australian television program, *A Current Affair*.

Each of the four sets of parents had taught their children that if they were home alone and someone

knocked on the door, 'Don't let them in if you don't know them.' In three of the four secretly filmed tests, the parents watched aghast from a television van parked on the street as the cameras rolled and I knocked on the door and their children let me in.

In one instance, using an approach I have learnt from studying the habits of dangerous predators, I told a little boy in a friendly tone, 'My dog got off the leash, and I think he has squeezed under your fence and is in your backyard.'

Two other children were watching from inside as the boy responded with, 'Yeah, no problem,' and opened the screen door to let me in. I felt very uncomfortable about being in a house with children I did not know. They later confided that they, too, felt uncomfortable but, after a few disarming questions from me, the boy took me to his bedroom, where he showed me a new poster on his wall. He then took me into the kitchen and gave me a drink.

When the interviewer from *A Current Affair* later asked the boy, 'Why did you let Brett in the house?' he said he knew the rules about strangers, 'but he didn't look like a stranger.'

While being taught to be wary of people they do not know, children in loving homes are taught to respect adults. When a scenario such as the one we created for these children confronts them, they are faced with the dilemma of respecting an adult person's wishes or being cautious.

The boy had created an image in his mind of what

a stranger looked like and how he felt one would act. I did not fit his profile. Everyone on the internet leaves a profile or a picture — true or false — in their readers' minds based on what they communicate. The reader is left with an impression based on the information they see and their mind creates the rest of the picture and convinces them it is true. Everyone can be trained to control how their mind processes online information. This comes back to understanding the nature of the internet.

A predator seizes on vulnerabilities to get through the guard of an unsuspecting individual. The technique is even more effective online than in the physical world, as a predator's identity and motive can be more difficult to determine.

The most commonly sought information by online users for initial contact with someone they don't know is an image or personal details such as age, sex, and location — all the information internet users need to create a picture of the person they are communicating with. In deciding whether they want to interact, they want to know details including how old the other person is. A teenager naturally would be less likely to want to interact with a ten year old or a seventy year old stranger. This is an essential question for child predators because they want to know if the person they are starting a conversation with is a potential victim. Now that posting personal photos online is common, questions are often no longer needed.

A detective disguised as a child needs to provide their alias details to continue chatting and, in doing so, is aware they are letting a stranger into their life. Fooled into thinking they are talking to a child, a predator then commences the grooming process. They instantly have a direct connection with their target's life and family — or so they think.

Informed choices minimise the risk of online dangers adversely affecting children and their families. Children are not always good at making decisions that minimise risks. The young person who loses his job for saying something defamatory about the boss in his social networking account 'knows' the internet is a public place, 'knows' that other people can see what he posts, 'knows' they can print it out, 'knows' they can give it to the boss, 'knows' he can lose his job, yet he still does it. He would not say it to the boss's face, yet he says it online.

Many offenders I arrested for doing the wrong thing online may never have done it if faced with the same opportunity in person. If people falsely believe they are in a world that offers them privacy, control, and anonymity, where everyday rules and laws do not apply, it makes it very difficult for them to make the same choices they would make in the physical world. Correcting the misconception that the internet is not private is half the battle in assisting children to make better choices. The other half of the solution is changing bad habits and reinforcing good ones.

One simple exercise to teach children is the 'Grandma test': 'If Grandma is looking over my shoulder while I say or type something, would she be proud or ashamed?'

Parents have a key role in moulding children's behaviour. They already mould their behaviour so well in the physical world that they make hundreds of good choices daily without even knowing it.

There will always be people who choose to do the wrong thing, even though they know where they stand; however, most people, most times, make the right choice. Children's online behaviours can be moulded so they know the world they are in and instinctively make sound choices. As in the physical world, they are rewarded by avoiding embarrassment, danger, harm, or trouble. Avoiding these consequences is the biggest motivator they have to make the right choices.

Scenarios parents teach children in the physical world are transferable to the cyber world:

Scenario 1 — When a person gets into a vehicle, they put a seatbelt on without even thinking. They do this automatically because they have been conditioned to understand the nature of the physical world and where to take precautions. They make the choice so often they do it without thinking. Even though not everyone has been in a car crash, they trust the information given to them as they are growing up, and wear the belt to protect themselves. We also put it on because we know

if we are pulled over by the police, we will get a ticket — it is a rule.

Scenario 2 — If some stranger approaches in a shopping centre and asks, 'Can you tell me where Starbucks is?' we have no problem in quickly replying, 'Yeah, it is three shops down on the left.' While they do not know this person, most people feel comfortable talking to them because it is normal behaviour in society for a stranger to ask for directions. However, what if that person were to add, 'Oh, and by the way, what's your name? Where do you go to school? What is your mobile phone number? Where do you live? Have you got a photo of you and your family that you can give to me?' this would change the context of the interaction. Asking someone they have met for the first time for personal details is unacceptable behaviour in society. It would raise the suspicion: 'Why do you want this information?'

Scenario 3 — When a girl stands in a shopping aisle, very little is stopping her from taking something off a shelf and walking out of the store with it, yet she does not even consider taking it. She was not born with the knowledge that it is wrong to take it. She has been taught that it is wrong to take someone else's property, unless she buys it or it is willingly given to her.

Scenario 4 — A twelve year old son comes home from school and says, 'Sorry I'm late, Dad. I stopped to get

something to eat on the way home, and I met a friend. He is really friendly and has just moved in down the road. We got talking. He likes playing Minecraft like me. I hope you don't mind, but I have brought him home. I was hoping we could play for a while before I do my homework. Let me introduce Calum. He is fifty-two years old.'

Every parent would understand when the boy's father does not greet Calum with open arms. Rather, a dad would typically say, 'Who are you? Why are you even speaking to my son, let alone coming to his house?' What Calum has done is unacceptable, regardless of whether his 'friendship' is good or bad or what his real intentions are. Even though Calum has not broken any laws, his behaviour is considered unacceptable in society. Children and other age groups generally associate with people in the physical world who are from their own generation. Children must be taught to take this mindset online. It should still be concerning if much older users are trying to associate with or befriend children online.

Scenario 5 — Two girls take fun photos with their families and friends on holidays at the beach. They take 'selfie' photos of each other in their bikinis, and when they are the only ones in possession of these images, it amounts to capturing memories of good times. Upon arriving home, one girl innocently posts their bikini photos on Facebook.

You don't have to be a detective to know what

happens next. An adult stranger the girl would never associate with in person often copies such images. If that same stranger stood over her at the beach, looked her up and down, took a photo of her on his phone, and uploaded it to the internet, she would freak out and call the police.

Many children — and adults — do not stop to think that exactly the same opportunity for deviants is created when they post materials online. These girls never considered this man could access the photo once she placed it on the internet. He has not broken any criminal laws, but his actions are concerning, and police officers would be interested in speaking with this adult.

Parents must transfer the same mindset used to safeguard themselves and their children in the physical world to technology. Children can be helped to understand it is not normal for people online who are not part of their physical world to ask for, or be provided with, personal information for no reason at all. They learned the nature of the physical world brilliantly. They make hundreds of good choices every day of the week without even thinking about it. They can be equipped to do the same in the cyber world.

Crimes and behaviour in virtual space have consequences in the real world. To make good choices online, the mindset of parents and children needs to be: 'If I was at the shops and this happened, how would I react?'

9
The One We Least Expected

Ernie was more aggressive than any predator I had encountered previously. The investigation started out just like any other. In the course of our normal online activities, we were contacted by a criminal. Before long, we observed that he was overly forceful in his approach. As my partner and I worked together to gather the evidence, we began forming a picture in our minds of how this guy would present in person.

Thinking he was talking to a thirteen year old girl, Emilie, he promised my alter-ego gifts and indicated he thought I was the prettiest girl on the internet. He seemed extremely confident. He was very forthright and tried to exercise control over me, his demeanour stopping just short of being threatening. As I continued to talk with him online, he tried to desensitise Emilie by forwarding indecent materials to her.

'All young people are doing this,' Ernie said. 'It is fantastic! It is great!'

It reached the stage where I could predict Ernie's next comment or question and sometimes I had my answer already typed out, ready to go. It became evident the control he felt he was having over Emilie, the images he was exposing her to and the indecent conversation he was forcing on her, was sexually exciting him.

His aggressive approach involved making it clear from the outset that he would like to meet Emilie in person. He sounded very experienced and showed no qualms about engaging in these perverted activities. He carried the conversation confidently in a way he felt a young person could identify with and would accept his advances.

As we communicated, Ernie showed that despite being blunt, he was more cautious than most. He wanted to speak to Emilie in person through a phone call, so we arranged for a police officer with a younger-sounding voice to talk with him. It was a short call but enough to satisfy him that he was talking to a teenage girl.

Why didn't the predator pick the difference in an adult voice? I believe he created an image of the online child in his mind, lowering his natural inclination to question the voice tone. Behind the scenes, my colleagues and I made the usual searches. We discovered Ernie's true identity and where he lived.

During background searches, we learnt he had already groomed a teenage girl online before luring her in the physical world to a motel room where he paid her to undress and walk around naked. He did nothing to her physically, but photographed and videoed her and gave her a gift as payment. Later he approached the girl again about engaging in similar activities. She considered it but felt very uncomfortable and finally said no. He would not accept this.

'I have got those photos and video of you from the first time,' Ernie threatened. 'If you do not meet me

and do this again and more, I am going to make sure that your parents, friends and school see those images. You will be humiliated, and you will get into a lot of trouble.'

All decent parents would be angered deeply at this disgusting predator's approach. We can only think of the hopelessness and despair he had instilled in the girl. Despite being cornered by his evil actions, the girl had enough resolve not to give in to his blackmail attempts. She told her parents. A complaint was made to the police, but it was later withdrawn because the girl did not want to go through the trauma of a court case. However, Ernie's actions were still listed in the police files and we were fully aware of his disturbing past when he eventually made the approach to meet Emilie in person. He indicated that he wanted to meet in real life and take naked photographs of her for money.

He asked Emilie to travel a long distance to where he lived to meet him. We interpreted this as part of his need for control. Emilie told him that was not possible, but she could get a train about halfway. He said he would drive to the station, pick her up, and take her to a motel. A time and date was reached.

Ever cautious, the predator again arranged to speak to Emilie to check he was not being set up and she really was travelling on the train. We were heading by car to the train station to meet him when he called by mobile and left a message saying he wanted to speak. As my detective partner was a female with a relatively youthful voice, we arranged for her to call back. I dropped her

at a different train station where she got on the train and gave him a call. Her youngish voice coupled with the background noise of the train convinced Ernie he would be meeting a teenage girl at the station.

While we travelled to the station, fellow officers staked out Ernie's address. They witnessed a car pull out of his garage immediately after the phone call and tailed Ernie from his house to the station. He arrived just as the train pulled in and my partner got off. We joined a team of detectives and approached his vehicle. Ernie remained seated as I walked past his vehicle and peered in the back. I noticed a wheelchair but did not think much of it at that stage. I approached Ernie's driver's side door and asked him to get out.

As he hopped out, I noted that he had no idea what was going on. As with most offenders, they still believe the child is real. They think they can talk their way out of any allegations and that no one else knows what is going on. Or they think the child's parents have reported them to the police after discovering conversations with their child online. Approaching child sex offenders and interviewing them when they still believe the child really exists is one of the best parts of the investigation. By then the detective has developed a watertight case that the offender cannot get out of; the offender just doesn't know it yet, so tries to talk the detective around.

As I stood by Ernie's side door and he got out, I was keen to see the stature of someone who had conducted themselves as aggressively as anyone I had encountered online. To my dismay, I observed that Ernie was severely

physically handicapped. I realised the wheelchair was his. He could only manage to walk with great difficulty.

This cannot be the guy I was communicating with on the internet, I thought incredulously. I had to acknowledge that I too had fallen victim to creating a picture of the offender in my mind based on whom he portrayed himself to be on the internet. As an adult and trained detective, I was used to doing these investigations. I thought little could surprise me when I stepped in to arrest a predator. Yet in this instance I had formed a picture of a very confident, aggressive child predator. In reality, Ernie turned out to be a visually insignificant and non-threatening person. The experience reinforced to me how vulnerable young people can be online to believing the information they see on the screen.

Despite Ernie's debilitating physical condition, I consider him one of the most dangerous predators I have arrested. Pretending to be Emilie on the screen showed me the darkest corners of his psyche. He was not only capable of evil, he had already committed the most despicable crimes. Despite the earlier victim withdrawing her complaint, Ernie controlled the behaviour of a teenage girl, leading her to engage in humiliating acts that she lives with for the rest of her life.

After arresting Ernie at the railway station, we took him back to his house and located the computer he had been communicating with me on. As with every offender I have arrested, when we searched his home to take possession of evidence, his computer setup and

the general state of his surroundings was different from what I expected. While Ernie was not short of resources, the residence was dirty, cluttered, and very untidy. He remains the most confident, relaxed, and experienced child predator I encountered online, and yet his physical appearance and surroundings did not line up at all. I found myself expecting to meet someone totally different from the person I apprehended. His arrest illustrates that what the viewer sees on their screen is just data someone else has put there; it will never be reality, and should not be the basis for personal choices.

Unlike many offenders when we finally catch up with them, Ernie was most defiant. Even though he was not in a position to pose a physical threat to his arresters, he was arrogant and uncooperative. He was not remorseful. His demeanour did nothing to keep him from a deserved jail term.

10
Exposing Strategies against the Innocent

Experiences in the physical and cyber worlds can be equally bizarre and the lessons we learn are transferrable. This is particularly true when observing how manipulative predators can be; how they even end up making the victim believe it is their fault. This is a key predator strategy to prevent their victims from coming forward and testifying against their abuser.

One of the more bizarre sexual abuse cases I gathered evidence for happened before I went online. It resulted in the conviction of a former police colleague, James Arthur Marriner. Some years before his indiscretions came to light, I spent several nights on the beat with Marriner in the west Brisbane suburb of Inala. I found him strange as he boasted about his distasteful sexual exploits. I was only twenty-one at the time and recall he wanted to be seen by people as a big man. His bragging while travelling around in the squad car turned out to be tame compared to the evidence that resulted in his conviction in 2003. As our night shift finished, I would head home to my family, and Marriner would head off to commit the most bizarre crimes imaginable. Sadly, Marriner's offences against the innocent occurred over almost twenty years before the first complaint was

made. He was exposed when two women he preyed on eventually got the courage to report him.

A lead investigator at the local Crime and Misconduct Commission and I were appointed to conduct a joint investigation. When he was arrested, Marriner was working as a sergeant at Ipswich, west of Brisbane. In the bizarre story recounted by the abused women, Marriner became involved with members of the Christian Brethren, an ultra-conservative group with strict rules that prohibited watching television or movies. For years, he coerced group members, ranging from age twelve to their early twenties, to take part in sexual perversion on the pretext of them being operatives in an undercover investigation to smash a paedophile ring. Sadly, the good, but sometimes misplaced, quality of trusting people is abused as readily in both the physical and cyber worlds.

Marriner enlisted the women and girls he contacted to run missions in a supposed surveillance operation he called 'Red Watch'. His recruiting procedures involved establishing identification records of the naïve women by taking naked photos; taking samples of pubic hair, blood, and urine; and providing detailed questionnaires that canvassed their sex lives. He sent them messages about their next assignment at night. One of the oddest messages directed a woman to go to a nearby park, where a briefcase was awaiting her. She was told that inside the case were instructions to a secret location. The briefcase's contents further directed her to proceed through the park and stop at

a red line Marriner had earlier marked on the ground. There she was to take off her clothes as the predators had special night vision glasses that could only spot her if she was fully dressed. Being naïve and not worldly, the woman believed Marriner and complied with his instructions.

On another occasion, Marriner directed a woman to fetch her mission briefing from a rubbish bin. As she searched through the bin, she was pricked on the hand by a needle Marriner had planted. He then told the alarmed woman the predators had placed the needle there and that she had contracted a sexually transmitted disease and needed tests requiring her to masturbate and provide a vaginal swab as she climaxed. He videoed this, saying it had to be shown to the hierarchy at police headquarters to demonstrate it had been done properly.

Marriner also rubbed a special 'antidote' cream over another woman's body.

In presenting the allegations of sexual perversion against Marriner, prosecutor Ron Swanwick said, 'These are the stories Enid Blyton would have written for the adult sleaze market.'

Mr Swanwick said the victims had been innocent and wide-eyed and trusted the accused without question.

Marriner was eventually found guilty of four counts of false pretences, three of assault causing bodily harm, one of misappropriation, one of indecent assault, three of aggravated indecent assault, one of attempted extortion, and one of fraud between 1983

and 2001. In sentencing him to five years' jail with no recommendation for early parole, Judge Manus Boyce described Marriner as devious, cunning, and manipulative. 'There is overwhelming evidence that you are a very devious pervert,' Judge Boyce said. 'Over eighteen years you have shown great cunning in manipulating people.'

Judge Boyce said the victims had led sheltered lives and were unworldly and vulnerable. The sad fact is that the members of the church involved were not hurting anybody. Rather, they were living the way they wanted to, and someone came in from the outside and took advantage of them. While Marriner would have presented as a less than ideal husband, his wife was brought up to believe you never leave your husband. It was only when her brothers and sisters and their children came forward and pointed out what he had done to them that they banded together as a family and reported him.

My perception after hours of talking to victims in the Marriner case and other crimes of abuse is that victims are often reluctant to come forward, and they tend to blame themselves to some degree for what has happened.

A further peculiar recollection of Marriner is that when I was a young police officer on the beat with him, I thought of him as being around 6 feet 2 inches tall and huge. Yet when I arrested him about seventeen years later in 2002, he appeared around five feet tall, and a small, snivelling man. This observation followed

through to my online detective work. When we eventually closed in on predators, the most sinister and threatening of them often turned out to be surprisingly weak in person, but dangerous people nonetheless.

To this day, nothing I have witnessed online has been weirder than the Marriner case that occurred in the physical world. When I began as an internet detective, I was confident that all of my experiences as a policeman in the physical world would kick in, in particular my previous few in a child safety and sexual assault unit. I found this to be the case, and it forms part of my message to parents and teachers to this day: people should draw upon the experiences they have picked up in the physical world and their protective instincts to protect their children online.

Technology will constantly change, but the fabric of a healthy society will not; responsibilities, beliefs, morals, ethics, and wholesome expectations must never change. Thinking regarding human nature should not change when technology presents new, uncharted scenarios.

Vulnerable victims don't know what they don't know.

11
The First Arrest

Pretending to be a teenager online and observing an internet predator's subtle grooming processes first-hand is brutally confronting. Negative emotions race as the detective comes 'face to face' with people under investigation. The predators reveal dark corners of their minds to the detective. When I first encountered this, I struggled to understand how anyone could inwardly harbour these illegal or perverted views.

The detective's strategy during these online interactions is to gather enough evidence to successfully prosecute. Often this is achieved by following the online process all the way through to meeting up with the predator. After the filth they are exposed to in reaching that point, detectives take quiet pleasure in the predators' surprise when, at an arranged meet-up with their intended victim, they are confronted not by a helpless child but by a police detective with handcuffs.

Sometimes, because of pending danger to children, detectives need to intervene before the meet-up. This scenario occurred in my first arrest. It involved apprehending a predator who intended to travel interstate, meet up with my underage alias, and engage in sexual activity in exchange for gifts.

Before revealing theses intentions, this man tried

to desensitise my child alter ego by exposing me to increasingly lewd conversations and content. Part of his strategy was to introduce me to his own fictitious teenage boy online. During conversations with the predator, I sensed we were heading towards 'the meeting', the inevitable collision of two intentions where neither of us were who we were pretending to be. Suddenly amid our online chatting, the man startled us when he disclosed that he was managing and coaching junior sport in his local community. That changed how my colleagues and I approached this case. This person already had access to real children. We needed to close in as quickly as possible. I swiftly advised my line manager and it was decided to move in, arrest, and charge the accused immediately.

The man lived in another state, yet we were apprehending him for committing an offence in Queensland. We provided a full brief of evidence to police in the man's home state of New South Wales and initiated extradition proceedings. We prepared a warrant for his arrest and forwarded it to the local police, who confirmed his location and address. A fellow detective and I then travelled interstate to visit his workplace with local police and take him into custody.

I felt nervous about physically confronting a person I had been communicating with online for weeks. It was a strange feeling knowing the first time I laid eyes on him that I would not only observe his outward appearance but know what was going on in his mind and who he really was. I was in a unique position

because no one else around him knew who he was when he thought no one was looking, including his workmates and the local police.

When a person meets a stranger for the first time, they never really know them that deeply. It is an incredible adrenalin rush to experience this degree of knowledge about a person's inner self. I felt as though I had total power and control over that person because no matter what he was about to say, I knew exactly what was going on inside him. This sets online police investigations apart from all other forms of detective work. To the other detectives who had not been tracing the man and his online behaviours, he seemed a normal guy. But when I looked at him, I saw right into his soul. I knew him better than his workmates did, and yet I had never met him. I knew him better than the closest person to him in the physical world. He was totally exposed to me, no matter what he said or how he acted. His online actions made him the person he really was.

When the accused was arrested, he had no clue that we had enough evidence to convict him or what we knew about him from our online investigations.

Laws and policing methods are being adapted to address internet crimes. This cross-jurisdictional case was the first of its kind involving prosecuting a person offending across state boundaries against a fictitious child. The ability to arrest the accused before he met his intended victim was made possible by new laws in my home state. Different measures have been

introduced in other Australian states or overseas to address online crime. The Queensland laws enabled a prosecution alleging the accused 'believed' the target was a child. We travelled interstate, arrested the man at his work, took him to his home, and executed a search warrant. We seized a large amount of evidence, including multiple computers, formally interviewed the accused at a local police station and extradited him to Queensland.

To my colleagues' and my great satisfaction, he was successfully prosecuted and convicted. This was a landmark case. Under the laws in Queensland, he was guilty of child sex offences and his intent to harm victims was deemed as serious as if he had been grooming a real child. The court's guilty verdict opened the doors for Queensland police to investigate individuals located anywhere in Australia offending against underage young people in the state.

The internet removes communication boundaries so effectively that offences can be committed across thousands of kilometres within seconds. One offender can commit dozens of illegal and inappropriate acts simultaneously, and law enforcement strives to keep pace. Loopholes in online use continue to present challenges for the criminal justice system. Human nature, both good and bad, continues to find new ways to express itself online.

Online detectives usually allow investigations to reach their logical conclusion, culminating in an arrest and prosecution. While it is a meticulous process, I

am pleased to say that my colleagues and I never had a case quashed. Because of the strong online evidence we gathered, and how clearly we established identity, intent and guilt, every case that went the full length resulted in a conviction. At times, the evidence was so compelling the predator, when faced with the 'real world' consequences, took their own life rather than face the public reaction and a prison sentence.

Law enforcement agencies and legal systems worldwide are still on a learning curve to determine how to best deal with offences committed online. The internet is not to blame for offences committed by those using it as a communication tool — people are. The offences still relate to people — offences against people, offences against the state — they are just being committed on the internet. Without the internet, an interstate offender could only groom a child by finding a way to become part of their physical world. To achieve that, they would need to travel to the state where the child is located early in the process. He would need a good reason to interact with the child, identify them as a victim, and then establish a forum to communicate regularly with them without raising suspicion. Then they would need reasons to talk to the target repeatedly, arrange to meet with them in private, groom them, and ultimately broach their intentions.

These sorts of opportunities to offend from interstate are virtually non-existent offline. However, a predator can use the internet to locate a person, commence a conversation, establish a grooming process, and

arrange to commit real offences against a child without ever having met them. The internet has increased opportunities for people to commit offences.

Internet increases predators' ability to reach children, making them more accessible.

12
Caught in a Web
of False Belief

The accused told the detective he was 'Cory, age thirty'. Both disclosures turned out to be true when police arrested him, which is unusual. Most predators pretend to be teenage boys or girls, but Cory did not.

Cory came across the detective's alter ego, Katie, among hundreds of players on a gaming site. The detective's methodology involved looking at how people were behaving, the questions they were asking, where they were going, and who they were pretending to be; he would ask, 'Is this normal?', 'Is this appropriate?', 'Why would someone ask me that?', And, 'Are they too good to be true?'

Predators act too good to be true, and Cory started asking Katie questions that made the detective very suspicious; questions such as: 'What school do you go to again? I think you told me, but I just forgot.'

Katie had not told him what school she went to.

'What colour are the school uniforms there?' he continued. 'I know some children who go to that school. I used to live in the area. I have got a Facebook account.'

Then, 'What is your Facebook ID? I am going to look at your Facebook page and see if I know some of your friends there.'

'What colour car does your dad drive? When does your mum get home from work?'

'Have you got younger brothers and sisters?'

'Where do you play sport on the weekend?'

All of these questions had one thing in common. They were about Katie, her family, and her movements. Cory had begun asking Katie for all of her personal information.

The detective kept thinking, *If this was happening in the physical world, would I think this is normal? Is it acceptable? What would I do?*

Katie did not have to answer questions, but she did. If she was a real child, she would have been making a bad choice. She told Cory about herself and her life, that she was a teenager. Then something amazing happened...

The second her message appeared on Cory's screen, his mind convinced him he was talking to a teenager. His mind would not let him believe anything else. Everything he did from that point on was governed by that belief. The detective pretending to be Katie just put a few words on his screen, and Cory let his mind convince him. Every person alive needs to be careful or their mind will try to convince them that things they see online are true.

Believing what the detective put on his screen was the first mistake he made. The second was that he thought the conversation was private, but whether it was or not was up to the detective. The detective shared his messages with detectives, lawyers, and a jury. Parts

of what he said were later published in the newspaper so the whole community could see it. So why would Cory think it was private? It was because he wanted it to be private; he believed it was private; and technology told him it was private. While the internet can do a lot, it can never guarantee privacy, and Cory found out the hard way.

Cory began talking rudely and indecently to Katie. The detective could have arrested him and was going to, when suddenly Cory wanted to meet Katie in person. He approached this by promising to give Katie something:

'Hey, I have just signed up for a phone plan, and they gave me a new mobile phone. I have already got one and don't need it.'

'You seem really nice and haven't got a mobile, so I'll give it to you.' He continued. 'Next time you are going to the local shopping centre, send me an email, and I will meet you there and give you the phone.'

So, Cory promised to give Katie something for free and arranged to meet her in a public place. If the detective had been the vulnerable, naïve child Cory thought he was he would not have known what the predator was really thinking. The detective appeared to fall into his trap. Katie could have said, 'Are you kidding? I'm not going to meet you in person. You are an adult. Why are you even talking to me on the internet? Can't you talk to people your own age?'

But Katie did not.

The internet is no different from the physical world.

People are still dealing with people. They are no better or more perfect on the internet. They are only seeing the stuff others want them to see. Whoever has had someone walk up to them in the street and give them a free iPad? What should someone think if they receive a message on their screen saying, 'Congratulations! You're the one-millionth visitor to this website. Click here to collect your free iPad.' Who is ever going to give away an iPad free? No one. A worst-case scenario might be that the giver puts a virus on the recipient's computer to be able to see what is going on, and might steal their personal information — anything they can find out about them, including their likes and their family. When a person 'likes' something on Facebook, they are profiled. There is a record somewhere of every single key a person presses on their computer that can be brought together to create an entire picture of them.

The detective knew who Cory was, even though the predator thought he was anonymous. The detective had his email address. He did a Google search on it and learnt that Cory had Facebook and Myspace accounts, and was a member of an online car group. He had been posting messages in an online forum and entered an online competition. His name was used in an all-school newsletter that was on the internet and in an online news article. Then the detective looked at all his friends on Facebook and Myspace and saw what they were saying, what pictures they had posted of him in their profiles. Yet for Cory, that screen made him feel as if nobody knew who he was.

Police followed him from his house to the shopping centre. He thought he was going to meet teenager Katie, but instead he met a whole lot of police officers who spoiled his day. He was arrested and taken back to his house. The detective had a search warrant typed out and ready to go. Police searched his house and got more evidence.

They found his computer, and when the detective took a look on it, he found 16,000 pages of chat logs, records of conversations he had had with Katie and other people on the internet. The detective read through them all and found many young people, both male and female between the ages of twelve and seventeen, that he had harmed on the internet, blackmailed, and exposed to wrong materials. He had managed to meet some of them in person.

The internet is not bad and neither are the programs most people use. It is how people like Cory use it that causes the problems. Parents should not be fooled into thinking people like Cory are not out there. There is good reason for parents to trust their instincts. This is about knowing what is and is not acceptable.

13
The Hunter and the Hunted

Learning offender strategies and the types of vulnerabilities they prey on helps detectives pick up the trail of child sex offenders. It requires studying profiles of typical offenders and their victims. People are not targeted by police for their sexual preference, but based on whether they are committing child sex offences. A person sexually attracted exclusively or non-exclusively to pre-pubescent children and widely referred to as a 'paedophile' is not guilty of any offence unless they commit an offence relating to a child by acting on their sexual preference.

As well as pretending to be a child online, detectives learn about predators by infiltrating their groups and becoming a part of their online community. They study predators' methodology, interact in their community, gain their trust, and identify individual threats and potential victims.

Some child sex offenders confine their offences to gathering and distributing illegal materials online; others try to meet their victims in person. Online child sex offenders include adults and, in some circumstances, children who — through naivety or with intention — create, possess, post, or distribute child exploitation materials online. Regardless of

their motives, their actions may constitute criminal activity.

Online predators are usually males, although they may be pretending, among other things, to be females. They come from all different backgrounds. They could be married or single; educated or otherwise; in high-flying jobs or unemployed; straight or effeminate; well-spoken or gruff; physically able or in a wheelchair; and in their twenties, thirties, forties, or fifties. The oldest I encountered was in his late sixties. While I believe I came across adult females online that could have been a direct threat to children, I never had the opportunity to establish their identities. However, women in the US have been found guilty and jailed for such crimes. Sometimes women are accomplices to male criminals. They know abuse is occurring but do nothing about it or, worse still, are coerced to take part in the crime.

Predators in the physical world often turn out to be a family member or trusted family friend. While the source of online threat is far more varied and can even come from the far side of the world, it can still come from within family. Complaints are made to police by parents concerned with comments or materials posted to their children by a family member or friend. They have felt their friends displayed concerning behaviours on the internet.

While boys and girls are both targets of child sex offenders, girls are at greater risk because more offenders prey on vulnerable girls. While perverted

men prey on both sexes, the percentage targeting girls is far greater.

Among the most dangerous online offenders are those who seek to meet their victims in person. They include those who are prepared to commit physical offences against children, if given the opportunity, and those seeking to commit offences against children specifically.

'Opportunists' are offenders who, while not looking to commit an online offence specifically against a child, are motivated by sexual drive and control, and will offend if an opportunity arises. They may seize on an opening to groom a child for sexual purposes or expose a child to indecent material. They may be prepared, if given an opportunity, to view, post, gather, and distribute child exploitation materials, or to physically offend against a child.

'Predators' are offenders who intentionally set out to commit online offences against a child. These offences range from committing psychological harm — by grooming children, exposing them to indecent materials, and coercing them to collaborate in indecent acts — to physically harm — by meeting them in person to commit offences.

A predator may prefer to target a child of a particular age group, gender, physical build, hair colour, nationality, or geographical location. Predators can be very different in their focus. Some target eight or nine year olds, while others think that this age group is too young or too old. Others pursue only girls or boys, while some do not care who they prey on. One

of Australia's worst offenders, Dennis Ferguson, who died in December 2012, stalked and offended against babies, either boys or girls. Ferguson saw eight or nine year old children as too old. Ferguson's attitude of 'I do not care, it just has to be a child' made him a very dangerous individual. It is not necessary to describe every offender's persuasion, only to say that online child sex offenders try to achieve the same sinister results online as they do in person when preying on the vulnerable and innocent.

A predator is more likely to offend because children are their sexual preference. Their motivation is higher, and they are prepared to take more risks. However, an opportunist is equally dangerous because of the effect they can have on children. Their methods and negative actions generally evolve as the offences take place and include everything the predator is prepared to do.

In the physical world, to be close to children, offenders join sports clubs, drive school buses, and become teachers. Sadly, society's awareness of their presence casts suspicion on the majority of people who serve in these pastimes and occupations. Online, the big difference is that an offender can strike from anywhere in the world within seconds.

Other predators visit dating sites to look at a woman's profile. Chillingly, the first aspect of her profile the predator will check is whether she has children. How many? Are they boys or girls? What ages are they? If the predator's approach is 'successful', they can be

invited straight into that vulnerable family's home. Dating sites attract many predators. The strategy is, 'I know that the children's mother is single and looking for someone. I know that if the relationship works, I can get into that home.'

While all predators possess common mindsets and predispositions, they can be very different in how they operate. Differing offender profiles use differing methods to target children. Particularly aggressive and fast-moving offenders can still take a long time to groom a young person and build a relationship with them.

Others come across as social networkers with wholesome everyday intentions to befriend a child and become a part of their life. Then they use subtle messages to try to obtain what they want. Those who are aggressive and direct from the outset communicate something like this to potential victims:

'Where are you sitting?'

'Can your mum see you?'

'Where are your parents?'

'Is the computer facing the door?'

'Is your door closed?'

'What are you wearing?'

'Have you ever touched yourself? How did you feel?'

It might sound far-fetched for someone to say this in the first ten minutes of engaging with a child on the internet; however, that is exactly what more aggressive predators do.

A normal child will most likely respond just as they would in the physical world with something like:

'Go away. You are disgusting,' or, 'That is ridiculous.' Then the predator will probably move on. Because so many people use technology, they can have multiple conversations in seconds until they come across a person who responds how they are hoping. Then the grooming process commences. Online investigators are exposed to these types of conversations thousands of times:

'I want you to touch yourself.'

'I want you to get a pen and insert it in yourself.'

'When you go to school, I want you to kiss your friend.'

When offenders use the internet to communicate these types of sinister activities, it dehumanises people. A child can tend to think that they are dealing with two-dimensional data, all the while not suspecting that they are being groomed for abuse.

At times when I observed predator behaviour online, it made me shiver with disgust. I did not feel instant hatred for those people, but I did very much dislike what they were doing. I never once lost my temper on the internet, even though I would have loved to turn around and say, 'Hey, pal, you have just committed a criminal offence. We are coming to get you.' That would have been highly satisfying but unprofessional.

Pretending to be a child online, detectives encounter every ploy imaginable from predators daily. 'Have you got a picture of yourself that I can see?' is a classic line from these people as they seek to find out as much personal information as possible.

Initially when they establish contact, predators want personal information so they can make their victim real in their minds. It heightens their sexual experience to believe they are 'doing it' online with a child. They are creating a picture, a profile of their victim. This is the first basic step they take to groom a potential victim.

A child sex offender cannot be identified by their appearance in person or online. A person who is scruffy-looking and socially awkward in person might be totally trustworthy around children. Conversely, a quiet, neatly dressed man who heads off to an office job every day might harbour dark secrets that not even those closest to him are aware of. No particular stereotype exists that will help parents identify an online predator or child sex offender in their neighbourhood.

The threat can come from anywhere because the internet enables predators to create false identities. What a person sees on the screen very often is not reality; it is just what has been put on the screen. A child may think they are communicating with a thirteen year old girl or fourteen year old boy, but the person on the other end may be a fifty year old. The only feedback often ever seen online is what is on the screen. It is about becoming conditioned to know that what is seen often is not reality; it is just what has been put on the screen.

Posting photos can help create an image of a person that is just not true. It becomes very powerful. Child sex offenders pretend to be the perfect internet friend, the person they want a vulnerable child to think they

are. In a child's mind, they also become the person that child wants them to be. There is a strong psychological effect, with the child wanting and believing them to be real. They become more real, important, and special to the child than anyone in the physical world. It happens with adults too. The stalker is creating a false persona in line with what the victim wants them to be. That is part of being groomed online.

14
The Five Stages
a Predator Follows

Even a well-taught child is not fully equipped to take all the necessary safeguards against strangers. No child can deal with every issue or situation in the adult world. It is not about how intelligent, well balanced, mature or IT savvy they are; they simply do not possess the level of life skills or instincts adults possess. Adults look at the world through different eyes. Predators use techniques designed to break through the defences of even the best-trained children, and unfortunately, the nature of technology provides the perfect environment for them to achieve this. Parents must be vigilant at all times in looking out for their children, both in the physical world and online. Knowing the five basic stages a predator follows will help in this.

Stage One — *Identify a potential victim.* Selecting a child might involve viewing their Facebook profile picture.

'That child is about ten, female, blonde...yep, that's the type of child I would want.'

While some predators are less discriminate, they normally look for someone based on:

- Age

- Sex

- Location

- Build

- Features (e.g. hair colour).

Most predators require some form of profile when it comes to a victim, however slight, even opportunists. It might be a preference for boys over girls. Those who require no identification profile are the most dangerous. It broadens their threat level if they have no preference but just want access to any child at all.

Stage Two — *Gather information about the child*. The predator delves into the child's life, visiting sites where they can be found. They explore what the child looks like in different scenarios through their social network photos. This makes the child real. It brings them to life in the predator's fantasies.

The gathering of information satisfies two main requirements of the predator. Firstly, it makes the victim real in their minds, often heightening their illegal fantasy or activity. Secondly, it helps to determine in the predator's mind whether a child who has drawn their attention is susceptible to being manipulated. Information collecting can include identifying the

child and where they live. These details can be gathered not only from the online activity and communications with the potential victim but also from friends or contacts' information.

Stage Three — *Identify and begin to fill a need.* 'Ah, so that's what they are missing — perfect!' They take notice of what the child is talking about online and what is happening in their lives on the internet.

A young girl might feel she is not as pretty as all her friends. Her low self-esteem is evident to the predator, who tunes into her self-depreciating communications, images, and posts. This gives the predator the green light they need to hone their attentions to this person. They take this opportunity to pose as a sixteen year old boy telling her she is the most beautiful girl that he has ever seen in his life, and that she is the answer to all his prayers. The predator's strategy is to fill the need of the young person, to show full commitment to the child.

The child's natural defences can be down because of the false sense of security the internet gives. The gathering of information helps the predator begin conversations that interest the victim. They begin to form an online relationship. They establish trust, credibility, and rapport with their targeted victim.

So often arrested predators confess how they were looking for an 'in' or a need. Predators look for young people who are dissatisfied with themselves and isolated from friends or family. Children who over sexualise themselves and readily share personal information

with strangers. Children who try to portray themselves as being older or who act differently online than they would for their age in the physical world. Predators have confessed to me these behaviours indicate a need or that the child has low self-esteem.

A child might indicate directly or indirectly they are from a broken family and there is no father in the home; they might need a father figure. Another child exploring self-harm might need a sympathetic shoulder to lean on. Perhaps a child and their parents are clashing in the home and an adult who finally understands is welcomed. Or a child is unhappy with their physical appearance — this covers most young people going through the pimples stage — and welcomes compliments on how beautiful they are.

A predator does not need to be told what a child's need might be. They can identify it by silently observing a child's online activity and behaviour. They watch, wait, and prepare to capitalise.

After pinpointing the child's weakness, the predator is perfectly positioned to commit an offence through grooming, threats, blackmail, or intimidation. Predators often get aggressive if they discover a target victim talking to someone else on the internet. 'Where have you been?' they press. 'Why have you taken so long to respond?' They become possessive and jealous.

Stage Four — *Desensitise the victim.* Lowering inhibitions is done by showing photos and videos and talking through inappropriate things online.

'Now play through this, and in just a little bit, we'll watch this,' the victim is enticed.

Other strategies a predator might use are, 'You should meet me.'

Or, 'We should do sexual things.'

'You're going to be left behind…All your friends are doing it, you may as well do it with me' is a ploy that makes the victim feel left behind and unimportant.

Detectives are required to keep the computer running and the video rolling as offenders think they are performing their disgusting acts in front of young children. One of my colleagues used to keep sticky notes on hand and would paste one over the explicit parts so he did not have to see it all. Even after all this time, I cannot shake some of the more explicit and disturbing images I witnessed.

As I engaged with these predators as an online detective, I felt the force of their persuasiveness, and it revolted me to know they thought they were destroying a child's innocence.

After viewing the depraved material predators expose a vulnerable young person to, it is inconceivable how damaging it would be on a developing child's mind. It would not only desensitise or normalise depraved acts, but it could very easily leave a permanent imprint in a child's memory. That is why this material should never be thought of as, 'That's just what children look at.'

Stage Five — *Initiate abuse, often including trying to arrange a meeting in the real world.* The offender

explores how far they can go in subjecting the child to further online abuse and may try to arrange a meeting in person.

15
The Fast, Aggressive Predator

he detective struggled mentally and emotionally with how quickly the predator was signalling
his intentions. Like most of his kind, he was trying to
source potential victims through an online teenage
forum. However, he was very direct. Rather than pretend to be another person by assuming a false character,
all he used to conceal his real identity was his online
nickname. He thought that hiding his personal particu-
lars would stop him being caught. While he was hiding
his identity, he certainly was not hiding his intentions.

Two detectives came across this particularly
dangerous child sex offender in an online forum.
They visited the forum often to work in tandem under
assumed teenage identities to flush out suspicious
characters. When one was lost for words, the other
would chime in. Working together also meant they had
someone in the physical world to share what they were
going through and they could debrief each other.

On this occasion, the predator singled out one of the
detective's alter egos. Fast aggressor, Lambert, quickly
invited the detective's thirteen year old female alias,
Emma, to communicate privately. Once they were in
a private forum, he fast tracked grooming Emma with
very direct comments. He was pushy, even forceful, to

the point of appearing to be jealous if he learnt Emma was communicating with anyone else.

Assertive offenders like Lambert can become upset if their prospective victim associates with anyone else. They can even become jealous if they suspect their target is associating with boys in the physical world, say at school. Lambert became possessive and domineering towards Emma online. Whether this was a real show of jealousy or fulfilling a fantasy to be dominant over another person, the detective was not sure.

Detectives learnt later when interviewing him that he would endlessly roam the internet using this forceful approach. Most young people he spoke to would put him in his place and quickly block him, but that did not deter him. He was looking for that one individual with an emotional void they wanted filled. He only needed to find one target with low self-esteem or emotional vulnerability that would be prepared to continue talking to him. He would then entice them to take part in his conversations and grooming processes.

For Lambert, online stalking and grooming was a numbers game. He knew a large pool of children were accessible through chat forums and gaming sites. He established contact with hundreds of underage prospects very quickly. He was not daunted if in speaking to twenty children, nineteen of them told him to 'get lost'; he lived in the hope that eventually he would find one prepared to communicate with him.

When he eventually found Emma on the internet, he

thought it was his lucky day. He began grooming her and in the very first conversation openly stated what he wanted from her. He promised gifts and tried to convince Emma the acts he wanted them to do were normal. This is a common tactic of predators on the internet. All child sex offenders try to desensitise their victims by 'normalising' proposed behaviours. They do this during conversations or by exposing the child to pornographic pictures and videos to convince them that it is normal to perform such acts.

'You have been shielded from this by your parents,' Lambert told Emma.

'This is what everyone is doing, Emma. People your age are doing this all the time.'

'You will be left behind if you don't engage in this sort of activity.'

'You are not doing anything wrong. It is fantastic!'

'Your parents are the ones doing the wrong thing.'

'You can talk to me about it.'

He encouraged Emma to continue meeting with him on the internet.

Behind the scenes, detectives carefully carried out background checks to gather information and evidence before making an arrest. They learned who Lambert really was and where he lived. They carried out surveillance on his home and then, upon his request, Emma agreed to meet him. The detectives knew he owned a motorbike and arranged for officers to tail him from his home. For tactical and safety reasons because he was aggressive, Emma proposed

meeting him at a shopping centre. Lambert agreed to the suggested meeting place.

'I am going down to the shops now,' Emma typed. The detective's adrenalin was pumping. This was it. He would be meeting this extremely aggressive person face to face for the first time and did not know what to expect.

'Okay, I am logging out, and I am going to head to the shops,' Lambert replied, undoubtedly full of anticipation too.

Lambert left his house soon after, police tailing him at a discrete distance as he rode his motorbike to the shopping centre. He did not look around once or suspect that anything was amiss. He confidently exuded an air that 'I am in control; I know exactly what is going on; I do not have to look over my shoulder.' An extra helmet was attached to the rear of his bike seat for the child he was going to take away. He had intent, he had arrogance, and it showed.

Police followed him straight to the shops where he had agreed to meet a thirteen year old girl, or so he thought. He parked his bike and headed to the food court where Emma had arranged to meet him. There he expected to buy a naïve teenage girl an ice cream in return for the sexual acts she would perform for him.

He arrived at the food court and stood exactly where he said he was going to stand without becoming the least bit suspicious that he was about to be arrested.

The detective who had been pretending to be Emma was waiting there for him with a team of plainclothes

detectives, looking on as Lambert scanned the court, trying to spot a girl who didn't really exist. He was unaware that police had created her persona to lure him into their trap. He just stood there, looking around for a teenager in a pink jumper with a logo on the front. He didn't appear to have a care in the world.

Lambert continued searching for thirty seconds before three detectives approached and introduced themselves.

The detective introduced himself and asked, 'Are you Earl Berber-Weir?' Police had already established his real name.

'Yes,' he replied, although at this stage he did not seem overly concerned.

'We would like to ask you some questions in relation to an internet user by the name of Lambert.'

His body movements indicated he was becoming edgy. No doubt he was wondering what else police knew about him and what they were doing in the food court.

'Are you prepared to accompany us to an office where we can discuss the activities of this online user?' the detective persisted.

Lambert's confidence drained and fear took over as it dawned on him that things had not gone to plan. His world was crumbling around him.

His responses became typical of offenders who suddenly realise the gravity of the situation and scramble for excuses. He muttered something about just being at the centre to shop, even though he was ninety minutes' drive from his home.

Lambert initially denied the allegations the detectives put to him as they arrested him at the shopping centre. He said he knew the person called Emma on the internet but none of the conversation was indecent, if anything, the girl was communicating inappropriately. He still did not know that one of the detectives he was sharing this with was Emma. The detectives took him back to police headquarters, where they interviewed him and placed all the transcripts in front of him. Only then did he acknowledge his actions. He finally pleaded guilty in court.

Lambert was young, solidly built, well-dressed, and clean cut. He was your 'average Joe'. He could have been that man walking by in the shopping centre. There is no profile photo of him under the description of a typical 'child sex offender' in any book on the topic. Disturbingly, he had been studying at university to be a teacher. During investigations, detectives found online messaging between him and fellow predators, who jested: 'How can you be a teacher?' to which he responded, 'Oh, I would never do it to my own students, that would just be sick.'

The brazenness of Lambert really floored detectives, and they later discovered why he was so confident. Before his arrest, he had already successfully used the approach to physically offend. Excellent detective work across several police departments ensured as many charges as possible against him stuck. Detectives from other units went through the transcripts and records of his communication with Emma. Searching his

computer, they learnt of many real teenagers and adults he had approached. He met some of the teenagers in person and sexually abused them. He took them back to his house, some more than once, using threats and intimidation. He involved other adult men to video and commit sexual acts against these young people.

Detectives realised he was not cautious because he had done it so many times before. Police were shocked by how often and quickly he ensnared the vulnerable — particularly young people but also adults. Some appeared to comply with his requests and want to take part, although his approach was designed to force their compliance by instilling fear.

During interviews with Lambert, detectives observed the psychological impact the internet has in confusing fantasy with reality. Even after he was apprehended and it was explained to him that he had been communicating online with a police officer and not a thirteen year old girl, he still believed a real child was involved. In his mind, the child the detective pretended to be was as real as someone walking around in the physical world. Maybe he was thinking the girl's parents found out and rang the police. It was obvious he was still thinking he could wriggle out of the allegations.

Long after he was apprehended, he continued to believe there was a real child and that the child may have wanted to rendezvous with him at the food court. He had no clue throughout his online grooming activities that he was actually communicating with a

police officer. His mind would not let him believe that. This psychological impact of the internet in convincing predators and victims their online encounters are genuine is widespread.

16
A Dangerous Lowering
of Inhibitions

One of the greatest challenges presented by the internet is its ability to lull people into lowering inhibitions that have normally safeguarded them. People used to write and post letters and send videos through the mail, but the time and energy it took to do this limited the amount of communication back and forth.

The internet has revolutionised information flow by creating a forum of instant access and connectivity, enabling people to connect at once with others anywhere in the world. Technology devices are becoming cheaper, so every house can access the internet. The internet is becoming more user friendly with programs being developed that make it easier to connect with others. It is being embraced in every area of life, and most of this is positive and exciting, except when it comes to those seeking new ways to use it inappropriately.

A person's mind is conditioned that 'seeing is believing'. When they see something in the physical world, their mind convinces them it is real, nobody can tell them any differently. When they look at a screen, their mind is still conditioned that way, and if they are not careful, without even knowing it, they are readily convinced that what they see on the screen is

not unverified data someone else has placed there, but reality.

When a person believes in their mind that something is real, it is difficult to undo. Their defences drop. They close their minds to other possibilities and make decisions based solely on what they believe to be the case. This is accentuated in a young person's developing mind because of limited life skills and is one reason children are vulnerable online.

The internet gives all users a feeling of being in a private place, where they have control and nobody knows who they are. This works against the potential victim (and the offender when they are oblivious to the law on their trail). The younger the child, the more vulnerable they are. All the screen information is being processed in their young minds and develops their definition of reality.

To test this, *A Current Affair* once filmed me assuming the identity of a thirteen year old girl. The objective was to explore whether I could entice a fourteen year old boy to add me to his social network site, how much information I could obtain from him, and how long it would take me.

At the end of the program, the interviewer revealed to the boy, with his father present, that the 'girl' he had been communicating with online was fictitious, that she never existed — there was no such person.

The interviewer then pointed to me and said, 'This is the person you added, the one you were communicating with.' I will never forget the boy's reaction. As he looked

at me, I could tell that he believed what he had been told, but struggled to process it.

When asked by the interviewer how the revelation made him feel, he said, 'She knows my name. She knows where I live. She knows quite a lot about me.' Despite being informed he had been communicating with an adult man, this normal fourteen year old was unable to say 'he' because his mind had convinced him that the online girl was real.

Children are excellent observers but not very good interpreters. They are good at seeing what is on the screen, but they interpret it with a child's mindset. This leaves them vulnerable to making ill-judged decisions.

An online predator is counting on children to make bad choices. If children do not make poor choices, they will be in a safe, controlled, entertaining, and fun environment. The predator cannot make a child type one 'T'. He is hoping that parents will not become involved, because they will help their child make better choices.

Certain dynamics online can have a profound effect on victims that were not so prevalent before internet technology:

Increased anonymity — Children can be more easily stalked by an enemy they do not know.

24/7 exposure — Children can be targeted any time, any place. Previously, they could escape to the security of their home and their bedroom, but if left unsupervised,

the all-pervasive nature of technology can now prevent them from ever totally escaping. Undoubtedly, this has contributed to a rise in young people's stress and anxiety levels.

The private nature of online communication — The victim feels disempowered when they are targeted because they feel they are alone.

Isolation — An online user can become detached from the real consequences of their actions. Like a fighter pilot who releases a bomb that kills hundreds of people, they do not see the destruction first-hand. They can push a button without really experiencing how destructive they have been.

The public extent — A person humiliated online is embarrassed not only among people physically standing around them; the whole world may be watching. They can never escape the global shaming. Even if they log off, the humiliation continues online.

These issues unravel the lives of adults as well as children. It is not just about what happens to them online; the consequences are translated into the physical world. Serious social issues can develop, the worst being people of all ages taking their own lives.

17
Offender from a
Respectable Home

Posing as thirteen year old Krystal, a detective was hot on the trail of a paedophile network. He was closing in on several men who lived in a town with a population of 100,000. The men were exchanging images and videos showing children being abused and were networking with each other to encourage and facilitate their illegal activities. They were conducting their illegal network via email, instant messaging, and websites.

The ringleader, Warwick, was frequenting online forums in search of vulnerable young people. Pretending to be a young girl, Janneke, the man casually took part in the types of online activity a teenager would engage in. Eventually, he came across Krystal. His strategy to groom Krystal was classic: approach the target, befriend them, gain their trust, and then introduce them to an older person online. Of course, Janneke and that older person, Warwick, were one and the same.

Warwick, endorsed by Janneke, eventually indicated what he wanted Krystal to do and promised to pay her money for the favour. He wanted to meet her at a hotel or take her to a suitable place where he would take photographs of her.

'Everything will be okay,' Janneke chimed in to reassure Krystal.

'I've done it. He's really nice.'

'He will give you the money and gifts.'

'He is safe. He is a nice guy.'

Janneke was trying to give Krystal a misplaced confidence and make her feel relaxed for the upcoming encounter.

'It's normal behaviour,' Janneke continued. 'People do it all the time.'

With Janneke's support, Warwick took a while to groom Krystal to meet him. Eventually, Krystal agreed. He was planning to travel a considerable distance to fulfil his intentions. It is not uncommon for sex predators to commit offences a safe distance from where they live; they think this will give them an alibi of sorts, and they are less likely to be seen by someone who knows them.

The detective and his colleagues knew where the offender lived and that the meeting point was in a different city. Through Krystal, they arranged to meet Warwick at a toilet block. Support police tailed him all the way from his home. On the way, Warwick withdrew money from an ATM; detectives discovered later it was the amount he promised to give Krystal. Perhaps he was intending to hand over the money, although these types of criminal rarely follow through. They normally just take their films and photos or engage in other illegal behaviours and then leave. Despite boy and girl lovers' claims that they really care for the under-aged child and

what they are doing is perfectly natural, the encounter is really only about them getting their sexual gratification. Promising to give the child a reward is their way of breaking down the child's reservation and coercing them to engage in very confronting behaviours. The child rarely gets the reward for their sexual humiliation; it is just a ploy to lure them out into the physical world.

When he was apprehended, Warwick was also carrying a disposable camera. It appeared that he was going to follow through with his intention to photograph the child and use the photographs for his own purposes. These may have been for personal pleasure, to sell to other predators or to use to blackmail the child into engaging in more activity at a later date.

When Warwick finally arrived at the toilet block, a team of police moved in to arrest him. He was interviewed and made full admissions.

The detective was not present when Warwick was arrested. He was part of a team of detectives who executed a search warrant at Warwick's hometown at the same time and took possession of his computers. Warwick lived with his wife and a daughter, who was the same age as the detective's alter ego, Krystal. The understanding dawned on the detective…this was why Warwick knew exactly how to communicate with a girl of that age on the internet. He knew what girls aged thirteen were interested in and what programs they used. He was using his knowledge of his own teenage daughter to pretend to be a thirteen year old girl on the internet to attract and lure other teenage girls. Detectives also

learnt that other young girls from the neighbourhood would regularly stay over at that house. The whole case became a very serious child protection issue. All of these young people were interviewed. Police acted to ensure his daughter's and the other girls' safety.

Warwick was aged around sixty. Teenage girls are surprised when they learn the intentions of some men at this age. 'Why would an old man want to have sex with young girls?' they ask. Their naivety is one of the best reasons for parents to be vigilant on their behalf. While teenagers often appear to be mature, they are far less susceptible to sex offenders when their parents weigh in with their protective instincts.

In examining Warwick's computers, police were alerted to the associated activities of other men around the same age who lived in the same area. They had been communicating and networking on the internet. They knew each other, not only online but in the physical world, and were using technology to cover their activities and conversations. Their communications included information about young people in the neighbourhood — their daily movements and part-time jobs. They even discussed the times these young people finished work and headed home. Each shared interaction they had with these young people in the physical world. In a bizarre form of networking, they would relate their experiences to one another over the internet.

As a result of the extensive evidence collected during online surveillance, the detective felt confident to move in on Warwick's home when he travelled to another

town to prey on Krystal. On executing a search warrant, police found the man had a fixed personal computer in the main area of the family home.

The detective learnt that, as well as having a teenage daughter, Warwick also had grandchildren who visited occasionally. Their photos were posted all around the house, and drawings they had done featured prominently in the offender's enclosed verandah. There seemed to be an unusual amount of these child-related drawings. Warwick may have wanted to come across to would-be victims and their parents visiting his home as a loving grandfather, or perhaps he posted things around the house that would interest a child and draw them in.

A further disarming fact was that he shared the family home with his wife. Even though it was never confirmed, it is almost certain his wife knew about the activity he was conducting on the internet but was not prepared to confront him about it. She came across as a very compliant wife who didn't want to cause disruptions. She most likely would not have agreed with her husband's illegal activity but, for whatever reason, chose to remain silent.

Initially Warwick denied committing the offences. That was until he learnt police had examined his computer. The detective challenged him about the obscene content found. Hundreds of images fell under the definition of child exploitation material, and police found online conversations he'd had with other men about accessing and committing offences against children.

The detective executed a search warrant on the house of another man involved in the paedophile ring and again found images on his computers depicting children being sexually abused.

Despite extensive investigations, the detective could not establish a physical world victim the men had offended against; neither could he find evidence they had groomed children online. This does not mean they were not guilty of further offences against children. Their intentions revealed they were consumed with meeting underage young people in person as evidenced by Warwick's willingness to travel so far to meet Krystal. It is hoped that police apprehended Warwick and his crime partner before they had the opportunity to physically abuse a child.

Common Predator Behaviour

- A common predator strategy involves approaching the potential victim, befriending them, gaining their trust, and introducing them to an older person online.
- Both online sex predators and those in the physical world often commit offences a safe distance from where they live.
- While offenders offer to pay money to their victims to encourage them to meet, it is normally a ploy to lure them out into the physical world.
- These offenders are often part of a network, communicating both online and in the physical world about real young people and their daily movements.

18
Learning to Value
Your Identity

Teaching children to appreciate the value of their online identity will lessen the risk of them falling victim to an online predator. They must be taught that their identity is very valuable and if they are visiting high-risk sites to play games, they should conceal their real identity. This cannot be stressed strongly enough! Users of gaming sites can use any program they want and still protect their identity. Nobody has the right to know anything about another person until they genuinely earn that privilege.

Imagine what you would do if you're walking home from school and someone pulled up in a car. They got out of the car and came over and stood in front of you and said, 'Hey, I just moved to the area. I like the look of you. I'm looking for friends. What's your name? Where do you go to school? What's your date of birth? Where do you live? What are your favourite things? What are your friends' names? Give me a photo of you and your friends at school.'

You wouldn't go, 'Oh, great. I've just made a new friend. I feel good now.' You'd think, 'Who are you?' You would probably turn around and run away. 'Why are you even talking to me, let alone asking me for that

information?' Why then would you feel it is okay to get on the internet and start sharing all that information with someone you don't know? You may have handed your details over to exactly the same person. You don't know. Do you need to take that chance?

Protecting one's identity online automatically follows on from understanding that the same rules apply on the internet as in the physical world. Nothing should change just because the communication happens behind a screen.

Children should not feel obligated to tell people about themselves while playing a game online. People are seeking their information for all sorts of reasons. Information equals power and money online, not only for child sex predators but for legitimate companies through to criminals. They require information to achieve their goals. Online profiling is an extremely profitable business. Companies use the information to market to people they know have been looking at products similar to theirs online. Criminals looking to steal identities require information. Predators or scammers need to know their victim. A person's identity is their property, and it is more valuable than gold. Usually for a predator to do the wrong thing by a child, they need as much information about them as they can get. Children who protect their information are protecting themselves.

Online users should conceal their true identity as much as possible and only reveal it where necessary. Legitimate information sharing might be for business

purposes on networking sites such as LinkedIn or filling out passport documents; however, there is no need to part with more information than necessary. Children cannot rely on the good nature of strangers to automatically do the right thing by them and their property.

In the physical world, children are taught not to divulge any information to strangers. They are taught to make right choices and to ask, 'Who are you?' and, 'Why do you need to have that information?' Transfer that same understanding to social networking and the truth is that many users are violating this principle by freely making their information available to strangers. Worse still, they are making it available 24/7. After a child has posted information on their social network profile, the site communicates that detail about them even when they sign out and go to school. They can be passing on to strangers the same information they refuse to divulge in person.

Rules of engagement are as important online as in the physical world. When messages are sent back and forth online, other humans are involved and boundaries need to be in place. It is dangerous to have a mindset of 'I would never let people treat me like that in the real world, but that is just on the internet.' Parents can help children establish healthy online boundaries so that no one can erode their confidence or self-esteem.

Children are used to rules. Even though at times they resent them, the boundaries give them security. School-aged children do not go to their wardrobes

each morning and say to themselves, 'Now, what's my favourite outfit? Oh, my school uniform. That's what I'll wear today.' Wrong. They wear their uniforms because they know they have to. They do not even think about it. Rather, they know, 'I've just got to wear a school uniform today because that's the rule. I don't want to embarrass myself. I don't want to get into trouble.'

Educating and encouraging children to value and protect their online identity is paramount. Instilling the right mindset in them involves convincing them their identity holds true worth. They should treat it as their most valuable possession. This is not to suggest they can never share personal details online; rather, they should decide where they share those details and with whom.

As a balance, internet users cannot escape divulging any information. No one can be totally anonymous. The emphasis is on ensuring children are aware of the internet's public nature. Technology provides the world with a complete record of everything posted. Many internet users would take back what they have posted if they could. Once 'upload', 'send', or 'enter' is pressed, the information has been delivered to somebody else. If something personal and private is going on in a child's life, the internet is the worst place to share information or videos or pictures about it.

A news editor cannot pre-determine or know who is going to buy their paper or how every reader is going to react to the content. They cannot turn around and say, 'That person was not supposed to read that,' or, 'We only

wanted certain people to buy or read the newspaper.' They need a mindset that assumes everybody in the community may read it. It is the same when posting or sharing information online.

Being cautious and thinking before making online decisions is essential. Information gathering and dissemination, for good or for bad, is the nature of the internet.

That is why parents — not technology — should determine what online activity will occur in the home. Do not be fooled into thinking, 'My child is thirteen, so he is going to get a Facebook account.' Parents should be making the decision in their homes whether their children will get a Facebook, Instagram, or Snapchat account. Social networking websites set the minimum age at thirteen because they require signed parental consent to access a child's information before then. After a child turns thirteen they do not require this permission. It is dangerous for families to leave this decision in the hands of for-profit companies. A parent is the best judge of whether their child is ready to use these programs. Technology must never be allowed to override parental decision-making.

Parents need to set rules and boundaries for their child's internet usage.

19
The Brazenness
of Some Offenders

The following scenario I was involved in could have unfolded in any city or regional town of Australia — or indeed the world. It illustrates how all communities, regardless of location, need to be vigilant.

Detective colleagues and I received complaints from regional police about a suspected paedophile network in a city in North Queensland. Investigations were initiated from headquarters in the southeast of the state, where we assumed fictitious identities of children and pretended to be from nearby areas to try to engage with these online suspects.

Before long, operating online under the persona of fictitious thirteen year old local teenage girl Charlotte, I befriended three men from the region. Charlotte established contact in online forums and communicated with them over a period of time.

Eventually, enough evidence related to exposing a child to indecent material on the internet was gathered to arrest them as child sex offenders.

A team, including myself, was mobilised to travel to the city to re-engage with the offenders online, then arrest them on different days. Setting up computers in a motel, we gathered strong evidence as Charlotte

continued to chat online with the trio. We teamed up with the local police, doing the online detective work and deploying the local detectives to confront and catch the offenders red-handed.

Everything went to plan as two of the men were arrested, but the third appeared to go offline for a while. Through inquiries, we knew a fair bit about this offender, Jack. We knew who he was, where he lived, and the illegal activities he was engaged in, but try as we may, we could not re-establish contact. It was reasonable to assume that he had gone quiet after the arrests of the other two. Then early one morning I awoke bleary eyed at the motel and turned on the work computer. I opened up the relevant accounts and heard the familiar 'ding, ding, ding, ding...' signalling that I had received a message. I promptly got on the internet and discovered that the third offender was online. He had reengaged and started a conversation.

'Hi, Jack,' Charlotte responded quickly, indicating she was online.

'I've missed you, Charlotte,' Jack said, indicating he had something on his mind and he wanted to have a chat with me.

'Would you like to see me on webcam?' he then asked.

Bowl of corn flakes in hand, I activated my webcam. When the device started up, I could not see Jack's face. He never did show his face on webcam. What came next did not surprise me, although I did not expect it at that time of the morning. I had seen it many times before during online surveillance...

It was only 7 a.m. and he began masturbating,

sitting on his office chair, filming from the waist down. I always felt disgusted witnessing these acts, but it did not paralyse me or prevent me from doing my job. I lost count of the number of times I would have to watch live, through webcam, as adult men masturbated and committed depraved acts.

I put my breakfast down and rang the local police, informing them Jack was currently at his house, online, and sitting at the computer. A search warrant had already been prepared, enabling police to arrive at the house within minutes.

'Can you see?' Jack asked Charlotte every now and again, as she had gone silent.

The lead detective was still on the phone to me when he reached the front door. 'Let me know when to knock,' he told me.

Jack continued to gratify himself as I instructed the detective to proceed. I could hear the knock.

At that exact moment, I watched on the screen as the startled offender sprang up from his chair and disappeared from webcam view.

I watched the screen, speechless, as the webcam continued to focus on the chair…now empty…left spinning in front of his computer.

Jack went to the front door, where he was confronted by police, ushered back into the room, and arrested.

One of the attending detectives then walked over to Jack's computer and typed a quick message to me.

I was still on the phone and heard him say, 'This is what I'm typing.'

What he wrote appeared on my computer, confirming that Jack, the person I had been communicating with, was the man they now had in custody.

Attending police told me later that when Jack opened the door, he was wearing a towel wrapped around his waist and was clearly aroused.

I had spoken to the offender a number of times online from Brisbane and formed the relationship with him on the internet that led to his arrest. At all times, he believed he was communicating with a young girl called Charlotte. During the search and arrest, I was on the phone to the attending detective. We had him. It is probably one of the most airtight identification cases I ever had. As with most of these offenders, the evidence was overwhelmingly convincing, and he pleaded guilty.

What amazed everyone involved in his arrest was that this offender was prepared to get on the internet and video himself masturbating in full view of a person he believed to be a thirteen year old girl at 7 a.m. in the morning. It seemed overly disturbing that he would do this at breakfast time. The offender was in his early to mid-twenties, lived at home with his girlfriend, and was employed in the city. He fitted the general profile of an online child sex offender: male, Caucasian, and aged anywhere from seventeen to sixty-five — not to say there are not offenders outside this race or age range.

The two other men arrested were also white males. One lived with his fiancée, and the other with his wife and children. One of the other offenders actually arranged to meet Charlotte at a local shopping centre

but did not turn up. We had all his details and a search warrant ready to serve. Charlotte had agreed a couple of times to meet with him at his request, but he failed to show. We are still unsure why. Eventually, when we moved in to execute the search warrant on his house and take possession of his devices, his fiancée could not comprehend that he could be guilty of these crimes. It is not uncommon for an offender's partner to be in denial, wanting to believe the best about their spouse. Sadly, spouses and children become casualties, their lives shattered. The man was arrested, charged, and pleaded guilty.

The actions of the third man were at first puzzling to us. We knew his identity and address and had all the evidence needed to be certain of his arrest. We had surveillance on the house and, knowing that his car was in the driveway, believed he was home. However, when we arrived to serve the search warrant, a car was out front, but the house was empty. We later discovered he was communicating from his computer at the house next door. The offender, his wife, and children had moved out of the property into his adjoining parents' home but still parked their car at the original address. It explained why surveillance indicated he was still communicating from the same locality.

Not one of the trio's convictions involved arresting them during an arranged meeting. Even though one made approaches to Charlotte about meeting in person, none of them really seemed to want a meeting. However, they were equally guilty. Each was arrested in his home

and successfully prosecuted for committing offences over the internet.

The men were prepared to psychologically affect, groom, and expose a young person to indecent material. Their actions, I believe, would have had an incredibly negative effect in desensitising an intended child victim. Each was seeking to identify a need they thought a vulnerable child might have in order to try to fill it. At the same time, they were seeking their own selfish gratification.

During interviews, none of the offenders showed remorse for their actions. They thought it was no big deal and they were being 'hard done by' for even being spoken to by police.

Despite the news of the offenders' arrests being publicised on the front page of the local newspaper, it did not deter other predators in the region. My colleagues continued to receive approaches online from others who, unperturbed, continued to roam the net in search of a victim.

20
Never Smile
at a Crocodile

Crocodiles populate Australia's northern regions in large numbers. To help locals and visitors avoid becoming a casualty to these dangerous creatures, the Queensland Government issues guidelines teaching people to be 'croc-wise'; that is, to know the crocodile's habits and follow guidelines that minimise the risks. In a similar way, knowing the predator's habits enables parents to become 'predator-wise'.

The human version of predators, like the crocodile, are patient. They will lie in wait for their victim for years, carefully concealing their presence, identifying the right target, and planning their attack.

Guidelines developed to safeguard against crocodile attacks acknowledge these predators are not likely to become extinct soon. Thus, the best form of action is to steer clear of their habitats and identify and take action early enough when they threaten. Similarly, predators are a multiplying breed, and while law enforcers are hot on their trail, the best safeguard is for everyday people to be wise to their devices.

	Crocodile-wise	Online Predator Precautions
1	Do not swim where crocodiles live.	Do not frequent sites where predators lie in wait.
2	Do not dangle arms and legs over the river bank or boat into the water.	Do not communicate online with a person who is unknown to us.
3	Do not feed crocodiles directly or by leaving fish and food scraps on boat ramps or campsites.	Provide as little personal information as possible for the predator to feed on.
4	If you fall out of a boat, get back in as soon as possible.	We all make mistakes online, but learn quickly and do not repeat them.
5	Avoid livestock and wildlife drinking spots. Crocodiles are patient and learned hunters; they know these spots are likely places to find a meal.	Do not be fooled into thinking sites are safe for children because lots of their friends are using them. It could be quite the opposite.
6	When camping at a site for a long time, do not form a pattern with activities, e.g. do not fish in the same place, at the same time, every time.	Teach children to vary their internet activity so a predator will not be able to follow their movements.

It is interesting to note that the crocodile-infested areas of Australia are highly inhabited by humans, yet

it is rare for a person to be taken by a crocodile when they know the habits of crocs and take safeguards. Equally interesting, local residents do not live in fear of them attacking. The people most frequently taken by crocodiles are tourists. They venture into the murky waters and threatening surroundings in ignorance and increase their chances of being taken.

It is parents and caregivers' responsibility to ensure their loved ones are not ignorant of predator habits and the dangers lying in wait on the internet.

Simple awareness increases safety significantly.

21
The Patient, Polite Predator

During investigations, detectives came across a concerning website called BoyChat that provided them with a clear insight into the mindset of adult men who prefer teenage boys, or younger, for sex. They refer to themselves, as do the police, as 'boy lovers' and are a very distinctive type of criminal. They appear to be far more committed than other child sex offenders, more focused, and harder to catch. They express their anger regularly as they harbour a grudge from knowing how society perceives them.

Before stumbling on their website, detectives knew these individuals existed on the internet, but it was extremely difficult to establish their identities. BoyChat gave them an online forum in which to connect, network, empower each other, and normalise their behaviour. Their motto is 'You are not alone', and their constant themes include reassuring each other that it is okay to be a predator and encouraging each other to embrace their feelings. The site encourages them to act on their desires rather than seek help for their illness.

Police used the online persona of a thirteen year old boy; let's call him Riley. The role playing deliberately displayed a lot of innocence, as would be expected of many boys Riley's age. Before long, Riley was

approached continually by a person with a different manner to the fast, aggressive type of predator. The new contact's grooming process was slow and methodical. This patient, polite groomer, Peter, joined a game Riley was playing. His strategy was to steadily grow the friendship by playing the game and letting it develop at a personal level.

Instead of hiding his age, he told Riley up front. Then after steadily communicating with Riley over several weeks, Peter began talking about topics of a sexual nature in a subtle and, on the surface, appropriate kind of way. He asked Riley lots of questions, probably to get a sense of who the teenager was. He was no doubt doing this with lots of boys, gathering information and trying to identify a victim. He then started to ask questions alluding to Riley's sexuality and the sexuality of others his age.

Eventually Peter identified a trait in Riley's persona suggesting he was curious about his sexuality. He began asking Riley about his sexual preferences. He was patient, but the detective posing as Riley and his supporting colleague had been even more patient; the bait was taken. The conversation became increasingly frank as Peter delved further into Riley's faked curiosity. He became more confident in probing that area, letting Riley know that he could ask him anything and he would explain it. He said he would not judge Riley like his friends and parents would. He said if Riley had a same sex persuasion, he should keep it to himself. He said he was really the only person in Riley's life at that stage that could be trusted.

Peter told Riley he was gay and that how Riley behaved online suggested he could have a similar sexual persuasion. He began exposing the thirteen year old to images and videos, initially of adult men having sex with each other, then of men with young boys. He would always make sure Riley was okay with it.

'I do not usually do this, but I can see that it may help you,' Peter said, making it sound as though their online discussions were all for Riley's benefit.

After a while, it became apparent to the detectives that the online discussions, and Peter's exposing of Riley to the disturbing images, were turning the predator on sexually. At one stage, Peter tried to coerce Riley to go to school and take nude photos of other boy students while they were sharing the change room. He wanted Riley to send the images to him. He said he could use them to explain to Riley the different stages of development in a boy becoming a man.

Peter gradually introduced an interest in 'maybe meeting', a face-to-face meeting in the physical world so he could 'explain' things further and 'demonstrate' some things. This was all a part of his approach to desensitise Riley and to explore whether there was a possibility that he would be interested in taking part in some of the activities he was describing.

During his grooming process, the offender also introduced Riley to another teenage male identity on the internet.

'I'm talking to another boy just like you on the internet,' Peter said. 'His name is Kai. He is fifteen

years old, and his sexual persuasion is towards boys as well. If you want to talk to him, that would be fine. He would be able to explain things to reassure you that you are normal, that everything is okay with you, and that you are in for a great life.'

Peter said Kai lived in New Zealand. It is thought he chose an overseas location to reduce the chance that Riley would try to arrange to meet Kai in person. While it was never confirmed, detectives believe the boy was a fictitious identity created by the offender to further desensitise and groom Riley.

On one occasion, while communicating with Riley, Peter said, 'Hey, why don't you send a message to Kai?'

'Okay,' Riley responded.

Peter then logged out and the boy Kai logged on, which firmed detectives' opinion that they were one and the same person. The program they were chatting in could only have one identity logged in per device, so it was not possible for Peter to have two identities communicating with Riley at the same time. Maybe Kai did exist, more probably not.

Still believing he was talking to a teenager, Peter continued chatting with Riley about having sex with others his age and with people of the same gender. 'Look, if you do not believe me that other children are doing these things, have a talk with my teenage friend Kai.'

The detective pretended to take Peter's advice and began talking to Kai.

It is suspected that the banter between Riley and Kai was exciting Peter sexually. All the while, Peter was

coming across as increasingly smug that he was closing in on Riley. His fifteen year old alter ego, or accomplice, was normalising that behaviour in Riley's mind, or so he thought.

Then one day, Kai dropped a bombshell: 'I have done sexual stuff with Peter!'

The detective almost fell off his computer chair. His heart started pumping as the adrenalin kicked in. The predator was making his intentions clearer, blissfully unaware that he was actually the one being hunted. Patient Groomer was moving towards meeting Riley in person.

'I have done these things, and I have done them with Peter,' Kai said of the obscene acts he had been showing Riley in images and videos online. 'It is fantastic! It is great!'

'Did you know Peter is rich? He will give you things if you are his friend like that.'

So, the groundwork was patiently being laid to make inappropriate activity sound very normal. Peter and Kai were priming Riley to think he could get a lot out of it. 'It is fun,' Peter said.

'It is exciting,' agreed Kai in follow-up chats. He told Riley that Peter would provide him with gifts and incentives if he had sex with him.

'That is what he does for me, he gives me fantastic gifts,' Kai said, still not knowing that the detective was certain he and the older man were the same person.

The patient, polite predator's methodology reflected in this case is similar to thousands of interactions

detectives have while tracking down online sex offenders who pursue boys or girls — or sometimes both. There is probably an even mix of speedy aggressors and patient groomers.

Peter finally expressed interest in setting up a meeting. He said he was prepared to fly to the region where Riley indicated he lived. Arrangements were communicated through Peter's young stand-in, Kai. 'Peter wants to fly to Queensland,' he told Riley. 'He will get a really nice unit, and you can meet him. Then you can do some of the things that we have been talking about.'

Peter's confidence was probably buoyed by noting that Riley had not objected to Kai's suggestion that he might pay him a visit. Peter's adult side kicked in. 'Riley, I have some dates worked out,' he said. 'I can fly to Queensland, get a unit near the beach, and you can meet me there.'

Therefore, arrangements were made for the detective's thirteen year old identity to meet Peter at a unit, but it never eventuated. During conversations with Peter, the detective came to suspect he was already physically offending against other boys. The detective and his online colleagues convened a meeting to determine how to fast track apprehending Peter.

When they confronted Peter, they did not expect him to react as calmly as he did, but this boy lover was a classic of that scenario. He remained calm as police searched his home and gathered more evidence. The detectives took possession of all his equipment. His computers and electronic storage devices contained a myriad of damning evidence.

In hindsight, there was a real likelihood that Peter would have followed through with his intention of flying to Queensland and renting a place to commit sexual offences against a young boy. He had the financial means with a high-paying office job. The case served as a sober reminder that child sex offenders come from all socio-economic sectors.

Peter also faced charges of exposing a person believed to be under age to pornography and producing, possessing, and distributing child exploitation material.

In apprehending him, police took care to abide by the laws of the state they were in. The charges made him incredibly embarrassed. All offenders know they have been committing crimes the community considers to be the most abhorrent it can contemplate. While the predator's actions reveal who they really are, they do not want to be looked down upon. Peter point blankly denied everything — right up to the point where he knew he was totally cornered and it was futile to deny it any longer. He fought hard.

All the while, the detective looked on knowingly. For weeks, he had been acting out the harmless child Riley on the receiving end of Peter's advances. He knew Peter on the inside better than anyone else in the world. Peter was in deep water. The detective watched as resignation set in. The predator's alter ego, Peter, was dead.

After the offender was convicted and served his jail term, police sought to return some of his possessions. Computers and other evidence are normally confiscated for good, but other items eventually not

used as evidence are returned. In trying to contact this dangerous child sex offender, police found that he appeared to have vanished from the face of the earth. They were only able to return the property through his solicitor. The property was delivered to a transport company, which forwarded it on to the solicitor's office. As far as police were concerned, Peter had totally disappeared.

These days, there is increased public debate on the release of child sex offenders back into the community, their whereabouts, and their predisposition to re-offend. I support increased scrutiny, ongoing monitoring, and serving of parole conditions as most, if not all, have a relentlessly dark desire that they seek to have filled.

Not long after Peter faded from view, the arresting detective received news he may have resurfaced. A fellow detective came across a person in an online forum who had the same traits as the offender who had been arrested and successfully prosecuted.

'Hey! I think I found that guy again,' the new detective exclaimed. 'I think he's back online.'

The detective had come across a person with the same 'MO' (modus operandi) as Peter. He used the same subtleties to carefully groom a potential victim over time — tell-tale signs that he was the same boy lover. He was interacting again with under aged young people on the internet in forums designed for young people. This time another detective was hot on his trail.

Peter had served his time, and while he was more cautious, he was now re-offending. The predisposition

to re-offend is common among predators arrested and prosecuted, found guilty, and jailed. No amount of punishment deters them. Detectives often see them back online, not always committing offences but frequenting the places young people meet. Others are never heard from again, with the process they went through serving as a deterrent to never re-offend.

The Patient, Polite Predator

- His strategy is to steadily grow the friendship at a personal level.
- After a time, he subtly raises sexual topics, in an almost appropriate way.
- He asks lots of questions and then gently enquires about to the victim's sexuality.
- The conversations become increasingly frank as he delves further into the victim's curiosity.
- He invites the victim to ask anything and says he will explain it.

22
Predators End Up
Paying a Price

Every one of the eighty-nine online offenders I arrested over a five-year period was compliant when I confronted them. Most of them stayed calm. I think most online predators are in denial about the seriousness of their situation. They never think they will be caught. I knew they were guilty because by the time we moved in to arrest them, we had established their identity beyond a doubt and gathered a watertight dossier of evidence against them.

Their reactions at first perplexed me, but I have come to understand it. If they were innocent, someone accused of serious sex offences against children would deny it and express anger and bewilderment at being wrongly accused and arrested. Yet the placid reaction universally displayed by child sex offenders when I arrested them did not make sense at first. It was not the normal reaction I would have imagined from someone accused of such abhorrent offences. I have come to understand that in most cases the child sex offender's initial reaction is one of guilt, even though they are in shock and denial — and horrified at being flushed out.

Predators consistently fail to realise the internet is a level playing field. Eventually their deeds will catch up

with them. With the increased sophistication of online surveillance, they are going to be caught. The false sense of anonymity the internet gives often leaves them oblivious to this fact, or too arrogant to think they will be caught.

Nobody receives preferential treatment online, and that includes those who choose to do the wrong thing. If the internet could speak, it might be heard to declare, 'Predators or cyber bullies, you have been making bad choices today, and today is the day that your luck is going to change — because when you post wrong materials. It is not up to you whether bad stuff happens, it is up to the user at the other end.'

Although virtually every online predator is compliant when arrested, this doesn't mean they are ready to tell the truth. They think they can edge their way out of the alleged offences and come up with an excuse. They do not suspect that online detectives know much about them. They do not feel they are going to lose their liberty.

As the detective describes the alleged offences to the accused and what is known about them, based on extensive evidence, they begin to realise the officer is in control. Their expression changes dramatically. They realise the position they are in and that the consequences could be dire. Their whole mindset changes. Their relaxed air of 'the detective cannot know what I know, so I am going to be okay' is replaced with a look of resignation. 'They have got me. I have been exposed.' They then become withdrawn, appearing to be very

embarrassed and humiliated. The world they believed existed only in their minds has been transferred into the physical world for all to see and judge.

There are rare instances where a predator believes he has a right to do what he does. A small minority — the most dangerous — are indignant and arrogant and will not acknowledge what they are doing is wrong. This mindset probably develops in them through progressive de-sensitisation or being empowered by networking with other predators. They arrogantly declare:

'This is how God made me. You and your society have made this wrong. I do not acknowledge society's reality.'

'You are the ones who made children believe this is wrong. I do not hurt children. I love children.'

In general, though, most predators know what they have been doing is wrong but cannot help themselves. Most appear to be very ashamed when confronted with the evidence. Predators who display the most aggressive traits online are rarely hostile when confronted in real life.

Arrests for online offences validate the need for online detective work. A detective colleague made one of the first arrests of an online predator in Queensland. A man fell for the detective pretending to be a teenage girl online and began an aggressive grooming process. Eventually, a physical world meeting was agreed to. Not knowing exactly how the meeting would unfold, detectives arranged to meet the man in a park virtually next door to where the online investigation was being conducted. They nervously turned up armed with

guns, and notebook and pen to take evidence. They also arranged for a large police backup. The offender arrived at exactly the arranged time and was arrested. He had not even considered that something could be up. The story of this early arrest was on the front page of every newspaper the following week.

'Online Predator Arrested Meeting Police', one headline read.

The offender believed he had been speaking to a real child. The realisation and accompanying look of disbelief finally came when he was shown the chat logs recorded by police. Now suspects are being arrested and charged every day of the week.

The community was sickened by that early case, but the arrest and subsequent publicity confirmed the need for online investigation. The case demonstrated a non-traditional form of investigation. The offender was arrested without physical evidence or a complainant. Until this point, pressing charges always required physical evidence, complainants, and victims. At the time, there was discussion whether a sexual offence had actually been committed, as no real child was involved. The perpetrator had committed virtual offences against a person they believed was a child.

Pursuing online offenders resulted in global cooperation between police. Not only were people apprehended in other states, as a result of online investigations in Australia, offenders were even jailed in the US. The ability to track down online criminals globally is a major reason much child exploitation

material is now run out of the Eastern Bloc, where it is more difficult to identify and prosecute offenders.

In one of the first interstate extradition cases, the accused was arrested at a corporate office and escorted from the premises. No one knew police were arriving at the workplace until the arresting party approached the front counter and asked for the office manager. Amid curious stares from inside the office, the manager was advised of the situation. He was told one of his employees might need to leave the workplace with police.

'Yes, he works here. I can go and get him for you, no problems at all,' the manager said, disappearing out the back and returning soon after accompanied by a large, blond, bespectacled man in his forties, well dressed in corporate attire.

The accused's initial reaction was one of bewilderment:

'Oh, what is this all about? Why is this all happening? I am a law-abiding citizen.'

Until that point, the man had no police record and no offences, not even a speeding ticket. He appeared to be a normal-functioning, model member of society.

The manager volunteered use of an office where discussion with the accused continued. During introductions, the man did not know what was going on. Then he was advised there was a warrant for his arrest. He had not been using his real name, but police internet investigations had identified him by both his real and online names.

'This is what is happening. There is a warrant for your arrest,' he was told, as the charge was read out. The realisation of what this was all about began sinking in for the man. He was accused of using the internet to expose a child under the age of sixteen to indecent material.

The accused's demeanour changed from bewilderment to mild shock. 'I do not know anything about this,' he responded, adopting an attitude of denial while remaining composed. He was advised of his rights and arrested.

The accused was a typical, conservative, clean-cut office worker who lived on his own. As often heard when apprehending similar types of defendants, he had been married once, but the marriage had not worked out. He could well have been 'the guy next door'.

The warrant was executed. The man was taken back to his house and was present as the place was searched. Then he was taken to the police station and interviewed. He was very compliant, quite chatty, and generally responsive. I took in the surroundings when we visited his home to gather the evidence. It was a smallish, older home, single level and built in the seventies. It was well kept with everything in place and a lot of technology. Later as we reflected, my detective partner, who was a female, said to me, 'Look at his profile, [from outward appearances] it fits you.' It was unnerving to acknowledge this. As the saying goes, you can't judge a book by its cover.

Until he was interviewed at the police station, the

man did not process the fact that his online approaches were not to an underage boy as he first thought, but to a detective posing as the boy. He was still convinced the online person he had been grooming was a child. During the interview, it was as though a light bulb went on in his head: 'These people sitting in front of me know a lot more about what I have been doing in secret than I thought they knew!'

Analysing the psychology behind his responses would be very interesting. He tried to explain that the online behaviours were not a reflection of who he really was. That was what some people thought he was because of his lifestyle though; he reasoned: single man in his early forties, a bit of a loner with only the company of a small dog.

All the incriminating evidence of his commun-ications with a detective's underage teen alter ego had been video recorded.

23
Family Member Caught
'Just Looking'

How hard would it be for a person who suspects a close member of their own family is a child sex offender? Detectives received a tip-off from a man who became concerned about possible foul play when he and his family visited his single brother. The complainant was in his fifties, and married with several small children. While staying with his brother, who lived on his own, he saw hard copy printed-out images of men having sex with boys. The dad said he was very nervous about bringing the information to police as the offender was his brother, but he felt he had a moral and social responsibility to report the matter. While he was a father and had his own children with him during the stay, he did not consider his brother to be a direct threat to his children.

Detectives never asked the man his motive for reporting his brother — whether he was looking to have him removed from society because of the threat he presented or so that his brother could receive assistance. Regardless, the brother felt he should report what he had found to police. There did not seem to be any good reason why he would lie, and detectives were confident that a search of his brother's property would uncover evidence of criminal activity.

Taking out a search warrant, they ran checks on the suspect and discovered he was on holiday in Thailand at the time. Again, knowing how relentless a predator's drives are, they flinched to think what he might be doing over there.

They learnt the date he was arriving back and, armed with the warrant, were at his home waiting for him upon his return.

The accused arrived in a taxi. As he hopped out, detectives introduced themselves, advising him they had a warrant and were going to search his house for child exploitation material.

'Do you have anything to declare at this stage?' he was asked.

'No,' he responded, showing no sign of nerves.

He was very cooperative as detectives searched his house and took possession of computers. He came across as meek and mild, not at all threatening, and remained respectful throughout the search. He also appeared to be very intelligent.

During an initial search of one of the computers, detectives discovered illegal pictures. Just as the complainant, his brother, had described, there were images of adult men having sex with young boys.

The offender stood passively while the search was being conducted and eventually volunteered, 'Look, off the record, what is going to happen to me?'

'Well, it depends what is on your computers,' the detective replied.

'There is illegal stuff there,' the offender said. 'Illegal pictures and videos.'

'Well, it depends how much is on there,' the officer said.

'There is a lot…thousands of pictures and videos depicting adult men having sex with young boys, or naked young boys,' he said.

'Well, it will become evident what is going to happen to you when we establish exactly what is on your computers,' the detective said.

The offender then proceeded to explain away his criminal actions. 'Look, off the record, my sexual preference is young boys, it always has been. It has been that way from a very early age, in my earliest memories. I can remember that I had a sexual attraction towards boys of my own age when I was a boy myself.

As I grew, the feelings did not change; they just grew stronger. The older I get, the more I am sexually attracted to young boys. I hate myself for it, and I try to distance myself from it.

I physically try to distance myself from boys because I do not trust myself. I want to change it, but I cannot. I believe it is a part of who I am, and it always has been. Changing me would be just like me saying to you, "Do not find adult women sexually attractive, find young boys sexually attractive." I just cannot do it. I try to satisfy my needs and my urges through pictures and videos.'

The offender's claim that he restricted his illegal sexual activity to electronic viewings may or may not have been true. It was never determined following his arrest whether he was linked to any underage people in

the physical world. Regardless, the man's actions were abusive and criminal.

His admission that he was doing the wrong thing is unusual in my experience in apprehending hard-core predators. They regularly try to justify to themselves what they are doing is acceptable: 'That is how God made me,' they offer pathetically. 'I do not hurt children.' 'I love children.' 'It was the child's idea, they made me do it.'

This man told police he knew what he was doing was wrong. Let's explore his claim. I strongly disagree with any suggestion that the man's actions are not as serious as offending in the physical world. Satisfying his desires through pictures and videos add up to an offence that is just as serious. The pictures and videos he procured depicting young boys being sexually abused are generally only created because there is a demand. While there is a market, children will continue to be abused. The man's sourcing of the illegal materials is as serious as personally offending against the children. By admitting that 'I satisfy my desires through pictures and videos,' the offender fuels demand for others to initiate and film the physical abuse of boys.

The question remains whether the courts would have found this adult man guilty of committing offences against the children in the electronic files. The man took his own life, just days after he was served the search warrant and before police could interview him.

24
Flying in the
Face of Conscience

J oining online predators' communities under a false identity gives detectives an opportunity to learn how these people talk among themselves — their language, their methodology, and what they are looking for online. These sites exist openly online, and while their theme is often close to the edge and enough to disturb all decent people, the content they post does not constitute an offence and cannot be taken offline. Parent awareness of predators and other peoples' belief and values systems can ensure more diligence in monitoring their child's online behaviours. Viewing just one of these posts or links offers enough incentive for parents to go straight home and put some rules in place.

These sites are created by 'boy lovers' and 'Lolita lovers', terms used by both the police and the people themselves who are attracted sexually to underage children. 'Lolita' refers to a pre-pubescent girl. The sites commonly give a sickening and twisted interpretation of what it means for young people to have fun. Site frequenters hint at the atrocious acts they would like to do to children. They give a disturbing insight into what boy lovers and Lolita lovers are thinking. The posts generally reflect anger at society. They clearly

describe their hatred for the law, teachers, parents, and other traditional areas of society because they are fully aware that society views them with abhorrence, and will penalise them harshly if they act on their evil urges and are caught.

Online predators do have twinges of conscience; however, these pangs are often only fleeting. A major reason for this is they turn to online communities that quickly justify their perverted and abusive sexual tendencies. The sites provide a forum for them to express their anti-social views and their outrage at being ostracised. These boy and girl lover sites move to support their followers' perverted outlook, thus desensitising their consciences. They empower their online communities by validating their viewpoint, regardless of how sick and twisted their view really is.

The following are typical excerpts from these sites. The content may prove upsetting, but revealing the types of content on these sites will motivate more parents to become involved in protecting their children online. Those parents who are already convinced and anticipate the content might be too upsetting should skip to the next chapter. Those who continue reading, fathers in particular, will be convinced to get involved as the content will ring alarm bells for every loving and protective parent. It is an excerpt from one of thousands of 'boy lover' websites.

BOYLOVE, TRUTH versus MYTH
The bilateral love between a boy and a man,

although it has a long and honourable history, has been corrupted in our time into something that is supposedly drastically harmful to the boy, and a perversion on the part of the man. Nothing could be further from the truth, and we shall attempt here to shed some light on these malicious myths that do their utmost to suppress the facts.

The myth of the boy lover is that of the man in a trench coat, lurking around a playground with a pocketful of candy. A shadowy, evil figure who is automatically linked with such loaded words as 'child molester', 'pervert', and the corrupted connotation of 'paedophile'. One whose only purpose in life is to force sexual activity upon any boy he can lure into his clutches. No one denies that these people exist, but these are not boy lovers, somewhere, somehow, something has gone terribly amiss, and they have become predators.

The truth about boy lovers is drastically different. They are people whom you know, teachers, neighbours, youth leaders, co-workers, scoutmasters, store clerks, coaches, citizens who are known for their care and compassion for boys. Men who deeply love and are concerned about the boys with whom they come in contact, men who would not harm a boy in any way. Men who are just like every other man except that they have been born with a sexual attraction to boys, upon which they may or may not act.

The myth that boys are not sexual until they reach a certain age is so absurd as to need no discussion,

147

loving and consensual relationships have nothing but happy memories of them, the friendship usually outlasts the sexual activities, and many remain close friends for a lifetime.

No further comment is required on the above content except that at any given time in internet forums children are frequenting, it is highly likely that a person with this intent is lurking, waiting to try to groom a vulnerable child.

This is enough motivation for all parents to be more diligent in overseeing their children's online activity. The more parents do get involved, the more they reduce the risks of their child falling victim.

25
Technology Halts
Teenage Offender

Towards the end of my time as an online detective, a colleague and I visited the FBI Innocent Images National Initiative Unit in Calverton, Maryland, US. While there, we were trained in a program that enabled us to trace people trading in, sharing, or possessing child exploitation material.

Upon returning to Australia, we began using this program in online investigations and identified an internet user who was downloading tagged child exploitation material and storing it on their computer. We took the time to gather the evidence and prepared the necessary documentation to arrest the culprit, including the alleged offences, permissions, an operational order, and search warrants. The information we sourced using the program enabled us to identify the premises where the child exploitation material was being downloaded. We did our usual checks to establish who lived at the address and learnt that a husband and wife lived there with their children.

Early one evening, we moved in to take possession of all computers in the home and establish the device being used to download the illegal material. The man was not home when we executed the warrant, but

his wife and children were. As we looked around the house, the wife directed us to a study where a personal computer was connected to the internet. A quick inspection of the computer established that it contained significant amounts of child exploitation materials — both pictures and videos. The woman contacted her husband to inform him of our investigation and a short time later he arrived home. He then accompanied us back to the police station, where we conducted a record of interview.

I was not prepared for what we learnt next. The husband never actually used that computer. Rather, his fourteen year old son used it for extended periods to access the internet. We returned with the father to the house, where it was established that the boy was the one downloading, storing, and sharing the child exploitation material. The computer contained thousands of videos and pictures depicting children being abused. Most of the images were of men sexually abusing boys. There was also a large quantity of male-on-male pornography. The boy was later interviewed by police, and made full admissions and disclosures about his illegal online activity.

What this boy was doing is probably very common around the world. I have no doubt that young people access this sort of material. However, when the police uncovered his indiscretions and his family, including his sister, found out what he had been doing, it caused enormous conflict. The boy had been questioning and exploring his sexual preferences, and this led to him

becoming addicted to the material he was accessing and viewing. It left the boy and his family with issues to sort through. The embarrassment, lack of trust, stress, and anxiety that fourteen year old and his family members felt would have been immeasurable.

Now, years later, this family would still be struggling with the events of that night. They must replay it regularly in their minds. The boy had committed serious criminal offences that an adult would be jailed for. Owing to his age, ready admissions, willingness to cooperate, and the fact it was his first offence, police officially cautioned him. Even though the offences cannot be considered a part of his adult criminal history in the future, they remain on his police record for life. The stresses the family faces as a result will probably last for the rest of their lives.

This case highlights the dangers of teenagers not only falling prey to online offenders but also becoming offenders themselves. The boy was not looking to hurt anybody. He was not trying to encourage the production of illegal material. He was operating out of curiosity. Did he have deep-seated issues already? Has looking at the illegal materials online changed him as a person, his personality, or his propensity towards that sort of activity? I think there is a real threat that he incurred psychological and emotional damage as a result of his activities.

His case highlights that the internet does not discriminate. It does not care who someone is, who their parents are, where they travel on it, how well they

can use it, how smart they are, or how mature they are. The internet simply judges a person by their actions. Sometimes it pulls things out of a person's mind that should stay there, thus releasing their true intentions.

A further observation in this case was really intriguing. As with any investigation, we took possession of any technology we suspected might provide evidence of a criminal offence being committed. When we confiscated the boy's computer — despite him being fully aware we knew what was on the computer — his main concern was that he would lose all his music. It was explained to him that we would forensically examine the computer, all the information on it would be wiped, and there was no guarantee the computer would be returned. It is astounding that in spite of the seriousness of his offences, his main concern was losing his music. Even after being apprehended, he did not fully appreciate the gravity of the situation he had placed himself in.

This boy's case is a prime example of how people can mentally minimise the seriousness of the activity they conduct on the internet. They think they are only dealing in data and typing with keys. To him, what he had done was not that serious, but the consequences were as serious as if he had perpetrated offences against children in person. Yet his main concern was that he would lose all his music, which was precious to him.

26
Children Not Immune from Prosecution

The internet can encourage good people to make bad choices if they are not cautious. Every child could conceivably commit offences online against other children. Children from good families have been arrested and charged for making poor choices, highlighting how rules and laws in the physical world also apply online. To guide children, it is important for parents to have a basic understanding of their family's and others' online rights and responsibilities.

Offences against children fall into three main areas commonly agreed on by cooperating law agencies around the world:

- Grooming for sexual purposes

- Creating, possessing, and distributing child abuse material

- Exposing children to indecent material.

However, investigations can become complicated when rulings differ across state and international boundaries regarding:

- The age a child becomes an adult

- The age a person is criminally responsible

- Names describing criminal offences

- A child's legal responsibilities.

This is a key area being worked through globally. Similar differences in legal interpretation extend to the legal age to drink, vote, go to war, drive, and have sex. In Queensland, a person becomes an adult at age seventeen, twelve months before every other Australian state. This means that a person can be dealt with criminally as an adult one year earlier in Queensland than elsewhere in Australia.

In addition, a person may be criminally liable for certain offences while still a child, with the age of criminal responsibility differing between countries, and between regions within countries. The following table shows how the Age of Majority (when a person is legally considered an adult) and Age of Criminal Responsibility (ACR) vary in the Western world.

The Age of Majority and Age of Criminal Responsibility Vary Between Countries

	Age of Majority (adult status)	Age of Criminal Responsibility	Notes
US	18	6 to 12	ACR dependent on state
Australia	17 or 18	10	Age of majority is 17 only in the state of Queensland
Canada	18 or 19	12	AOM dependent on province or territory
New Zealand	20	12 to 14	ACR dependent on type of offence
England	18	10	
South Africa	18	10	

Many countries, states, provinces, and territories only enact the ACR for certain offences and circumstances. Depending on the seriousness attached to an offence, the agreed age of responsibility is significant in determining the level of punishment or establishing a child understands right and wrong. The ACR in Australia is ten. This means that when someone turns ten, they can be arrested for a criminal offence. Recently, in a local newspaper, a ten year old was arrested for allegedly lighting a fire. In Queensland, arson, murder,

and rape are considered the 'big three offences'. An offender convicted of arson can be sentenced to life in prison, and the boy was arrested for the alleged offence.

However, most children are not arrested for doing the wrong thing because the poor choices they make normally are not that serious. When the offences are not that sinister, parents and authorities can help children learn from the experience. Solutions can be found by working together within the family, as a community and in school. That flexibility is invaluable. Child crime is different from adult crime. In most legal systems, child offenders are not considered to be fully conscious, moral individuals. As such, it is widely considered the best way to deal with them is to rehabilitate rather than punish them.

Parents and communities should know, and so should their children, that it is possible for them to face legal consequences for wrong choices online. While it is sobering to have to educate the young about the consequences of their actions, these laws rightly send the message that offences such as distributing child abuse material or exposing other children to indecent material are serious. Similarly, online bullying is not an option.

On reaching the age of criminal responsibility, a child can be held criminally accountable for their actions. Their community says that a child can be prosecuted for committing a criminal offence. While the minimum age of responsibility can vary and some

jurisdictions even raise or lower the age on occasions, it is important that parents teach the implications to children. Communities around the world have settled, with or without conditions, on an ACR ranging from ten to fifteen. Once a child reaches this age, they are subject to criminal or juvenile consequences. If the ACR in a community is ten, children should be told that when they reach this age, the consequences of their actions can be serious.

Jurisdictions with an ACR of ten include England, South Africa, Wales, Switzerland, and Australia (including federal, state, and territories). In the US, the age of criminal responsibility for federal offences is eleven and varies from six to twelve through most states, while some states do not have a minimum age. In New Zealand, it is between age ten and twelve depending on the crime. Other countries set the age as low as six, and others as high as eighteen. Communities can debate whether they agree with a particular age, but this does not change the fact that parents and children are bound by the age of responsibility applying in their respective communities.

Parents must also be aware that when their children make choices online, they may be subject to the laws, including age of responsibility, that apply in other communities worldwide, whether they are physically there or not. The best rule of thumb is to trust their instincts and teach their children well. The important point to remember is that even though a child is not classified as an adult for criminal purposes, they may

still be prosecuted for committing offences once they reach the age of criminal responsibility, they are just not treated as an adult offender.

Many anomalies exist in applying the law across jurisdictions. The finer details on legal liability should be verified through reliable professional sources in each region. So many variables exist relating to the wording of offences, the jurisdictional requirements, adult and child definitions, and the age of criminal responsibility. However, in many countries and jurisdictions around the world, a common thread is the protection of children from sexual offences and the punishment of those who choose to abuse children or operate outside public expectations.

Ignorance Is Not a Defence

- Parents are advised to research the laws relating to their and their child's online rights and responsibilities.
- In most communities around the world, the age of criminal responsibility ranges from 10 to 15.
- Children must be taught that the consequences of their actions can be serious once they reach this age.

27
Knowledge Coupled
with Common Sense

If in doubt about the varying legislation between jurisdictions, parents should err on the side of caution. It is dangerous for both children and adults to be involved with child exploitation materials. Communities do not minimise the seriousness of possessing these materials; neither do communities think it is funny when children deal in these images and videos. Coupling knowledge and common sense can make the difference. Everyone knows right from wrong. When parents and children make choices based on good faith, the risk of serious online behaviour issues is minimised.

Unless parents really want to research the federal and state legislation, I recommend going by an old-fashioned rule of thumb: 'If my grandparents or my parents were watching me do this, I would not do it, so I am not going to do it on the internet.' If a family applies this approach, they should be okay.

Let's examine how the following legal examples would be interpreted:

1. A person who knowingly possesses child pornography is guilty of an offence.

This law does not differentiate due to age, instead using the words 'a person' and applies to all community members equally once they have reached the age of criminal responsibility. If that age in a community is ten, a ten year old boy or girl can be dealt with criminally for possessing child abuse material. If an eleven year old boy photographs his genitals and forwards this via the internet to a fourteen year old girl, he may have committed serious criminal offences relating to 'producing child exploitation material', 'possessing child exploitation material', and 'distributing child exploitation material'. It would need to be determined whether these offences were enacted to target the girl.

2. An adult person who intentionally procures a child for unlawful sexual activity is guilty of an offence.

This offence can only be committed by someone coming under the local definition of an adult person. It also specifies that the offence can only be committed against a child, whatever that jurisdictional definition may be.

3. Any adult who exposes a person under the age of sixteen years to any indecent matter commits a felony (that is, a serious offence).

This again relates to an adult person as the perpetrator but nominates an age bracket for the victim. Even though the definition of a child in that jurisdiction may be eighteen or younger, this offence relates only to victims fifteen years or younger.

It would be beneficial to reach a more common

agreement on the law, its terminology and application across state, national and international jurisdictions. Many, me included, think the term 'child pornography' should be universally removed from the vocabulary. Much pornography is legal and provides sexual stimulation for an adult market. Placing the word 'child' in front, associates 'child pornography' with a legal product, detracting from the seriousness of the offence. It sexualises the child rather than denotes that the child has been exploited, assaulted, humiliated, and degraded. No doubt is left using the words 'exploitation' and 'abuse'. INTERPOL, the non-governmental international criminal police organisation facilitating international police cooperation, advocates using 'child exploitation materials' (CEM) as the appropriate terminology.

Sexting heads the list of offences committed against and by children. Sexting is the distribution of sexually explicit material, generally of oneself, to another using technology. It can include simple word-based messages, images, videos, or more than one of these. The term originally related to text messaging between phones but has been expanded to include the internet and telecommunication. The result is the same regardless of the device.

The following scenario illustrates how easy it is for children to become caught up in committing these serious offences.

Take a thirteen year old boy photographing himself naked, exposing his genitals. He has produced and also

possesses child exploitation material. He then sends this image to a fourteen year old girl via the internet. He has distributed child exploitation material. If the girl views and keeps that image, she now possesses child exploitation material. If she copies the image, she has produced child exploitation material, and if she sends it, she has distributed the material. These offences are regarded as extremely serious in many communities and offenders are dealt with harshly. Of course, it is assumed that these children have reached the age of criminal responsibility. Other offences may have been committed, including misuse of telecommunication or internet services.

The scenario just described occurs often among the young in communities. It is a real possibility that if complaints are made or these activities reported a child will face prosecution. Children are being arrested daily for these types of offences. The only way adults and children can guarantee they will not go down that path is to not engage in the activity. The legal, social, and educational damage that arises from sexting can be devastating for all involved. Like child sex offenders, no student imagines it is going to be them sitting in a police station.

A child who has illegal pictures, photographs, and images of somebody under age seventeen — in other words, child exploitation material — can be arrested for having just one of those photos on their phone. A person's digital footprint is a trail. Every photo they take or receive, every message they send, and everything they post becomes part of their digital footprint. Leave it anywhere on the internet and it provides the online

world with a complete record to assess who that person is, not who they really are.

A young candidate for the police force was surprised when his application was knocked back because earlier in his life he joined a particular online group. 'I never went to that group,' the applicant said. 'I did not know anyone else in it, I had no interest in it, and I did not know what it was.' It was explained to him that a photo of a marijuana leaf featured prominently on the group's website. He said he did not even know what it was at the time. He 'just joined this group', and that was the reason he was not selected for the police force.

Despite the ruling seeming unfair, say the applicant had been admitted to the force, became a detective, and arrested someone for a drug offence. He is sitting in the witness box, and the lawyer representing the accused says, 'We have done research on you on the internet and we found that when you were in school, you associated yourself with an illegal drug. How good is your credibility now you are actually arresting my client for the same thing?' The candidate had blown his credibility with one careless online act.

A twelve year old might send a pornographic image to a younger student. When the child sees it, they might find it interesting, laugh, then delete it; or they may do the right thing and show their parents, and the next day, the police will visit the school. A Year 12 student at a private school was arrested for this illegal act. His whole world has changed. He was instantly expelled, and at last report was reporting on bail pending his trial.

28
Internet Makes the
World Smaller

I was among the first Australian online detectives to establish relations with US law enforcement agencies, with whom we forged strong and cooperative relationships. In now promoting safer online practices and parental involvement, I regularly contact my American counterparts to keep abreast of trends there. One of the first local cases that affirmed the need for more international cooperation between online agencies involved a US citizen caught offending in regional Australia.

Ted assumed the fictitious identify of a teenager who lived in an Australian town. He started communicating with detectives in a forum for teenagers, initially engaging in routine conversation. Detectives led him to believe he was talking to thirteen year old Anna. Like all predators, Ted raised police interest through his comments and the information he was trying to solicit. Key signals included the extreme interest he took in Anna. Out of all the billions of people on the internet, Ted treated her as someone special. He tried to generate trust in the relationship and build rapport. He was very interested in personal details and nearly instantly asked for photographs. He took the conversation offline to a more private instant messaging program where he

hoped Anna could communicate more effectively and exchange photos.

'What are you wearing?' he asked

'Are you in your room?'

'Where are your parents?'

'Is the door of your room closed?'

Detectives communicated with Ted for weeks as his grooming process continued. It raised their interest when he asked Anna for photos so he could make her real in his mind. He then asked if she had ever masturbated. When Anna told him she did not know what that was all about, he said he wanted to describe it to her. He wanted Anna to touch herself while he was explaining how to masturbate.

'Everyone does it, and it is normal,' he said.

Ted wanted Anna to insert her fingers into herself and suggested that she source objects in the bedroom to use on herself. He communicated this way with her for weeks. As much as he persisted in trying to get her to do it, the detective made excuses why Anna could not. She would excuse herself from the conversation and the communication would resume the next day. Police continued to gather evidence against Ted; he was committing multiple offences through the content he shared in conversations, believing he was talking to a child. The offences centred on what he was exposing Anna to and asking her to do.

Ted lived a long way from Anna, so a team of detectives was assigned to go there and arrest him. Anna told him she was going there on holidays, but

attempts to meet Ted in person did not fall easily into place. His excuses ranged from the time not being right to he was going to be away. These are a typical predator's precautions to try to ensure they are not being investigated. Ted kept expressing his interest in meeting in person. Detectives wanted to close the operation down and remove him from society. They felt that because of the way he was communicating with Anna on the internet, other children may be at risk.

Eventually the team travelled to his community and intercepted him. Ted made no admissions because he thought nobody could possibly have anything on him. He still believed he had been communicating with a real child. The detective team searched his house and seized his computer equipment for forensic examination. Ted was escorted to the police station, interviewed, and charged.

Investigations established that he was visiting Australia on an education visa and studying for a Masters in Marine Archaeology on a scholarship. Police seized his US passport and learnt he had recently entered Australia. More internet searches into his background revealed he was a convicted sex offender in the US. There, communities are made aware of who sex offenders are, where they are, and what their offences were — unlike in Australia, where at the time of writing only Western Australia allows limited release of this type of information in certain circumstances. Detectives found a State of Illinois website containing

a photograph, full description and background on the offender, including the offences he had committed. The target was a registered sex offender there — arrested for trying to meet a child for illegal purposes. The 'child' he had established contact with on the internet in Illinois had turned out to be an undercover police officer.

Queensland police were astounded to learn Ted had offended in America, travelled to Australia, and tried to do the same here. Inquiries also found that he had declared his conviction on his visa. The relevant government authorities were aware of the conviction, granted him entry to Australia but failed to notify law enforcement.

Ted was held in custody until his court appearance. A deal was struck that he would plead guilty, immediately be taken into the custody of federal officials, and deported back to the US. He left, hopefully never to set foot on Australian soil again.

Ted presented as a pleasant person. His house was tidy. He was in his early twenties, a tanned Caucasian, fit, well educated, and well spoken. He rode a motor bike, lived in a rented two-story home, and had a bird in a cage. At all times in dealing with the police, he was polite and cooperative. On the exterior, no one would have suspected what was going on in his mind. It is baffling to see well-presented individuals wired like Ted who choose to target children when they could legally go on the internet and engage in the same sort of activity with females or males of legal age.

Detectives regularly come across adults on the internet who ask how old they are. When a detective responds that they are a child, most adults will comment: 'Oh, sorry, I did not realise you were that young. You should not be visiting this site'; 'You have got to be careful'; or, 'I am looking for people my own age'. It is no excuse for an adult with sexual intentions online to excuse their actions with, 'I just came across a child. I was not looking for a child.' It is no coincidence that Ted was arrested in both America and Australia while looking for a child. Children were his preference.

A forensic examination of his computer did not indicate he had been online meeting any adult women. As always with these investigations, arrested predators are frequenting places on the internet where teenagers or younger children go. This indicates a mindset that 'I am looking to connect with young children or teenagers, people who are not part of my generation.'

Predators Come from All Walks of Life

- This predator presented as an attractive person, had a very tidy house, and was in his early 20s, a tanned Caucasian, fit, well-educated, and well spoken.

- He rode a motor bike, lived in a rented two-story home, and had a bird in a cage. At all times in dealing with the police, he was polite and cooperative.

- On the exterior, no one would have suspected the thoughts going on in his mind.

29
In Search of
Holistic Answers

Building relationships with US online police, learning their systems, and interacting with their task forces enabled me to observe they wrestle with the same issues to effectively apprehend predators. I visited San Jose Police Force in California's Silicon Valley and attended a Silicon Valley Crime Against Children Conference. I also visited the Innocent Images National Initiative Unit (IINI) operated by the Federal Bureau of Intelligence (FBI) in Maryland before returning to spend more time with the San Jose City Police. IINI, a part of the FBI Cyber Division, is a nationwide initiative to combat online child sexual exploitation in the US. IINI's mission is to find and deter bad guys, and protect children online. It provides centralised coordination and analysis of national and international case information between state, local and international governments, and FBI field offices and legal attaches. IINI focuses on:

- Producers of child pornography

- Online organisations, enterprises, and communities that exploit children for profit or personal gain

- Major distributors of child pornography, such as those appearing to have transmitted a large volume of child pornography online on several occasions to several other people

- Individuals who travel, or indicate a willingness to travel, to engage in sexual activity with a minor.

The FBI operates a world team that specialises in tracking online predators globally. It kindly provided us with specialised software to use in investigations upon returning to Australia.

The US has been well ahead of Australia in addressing online paedophilia, not so much in intelligence measures but in acknowledging the seriousness of the issue and devoting resources and personnel to the task. The San Jose police were pleased to meet Australians involved in the same internet investigative work on the other side of the world. On a subsequent trip, I visited the Department of Homeland Security in Virginia and attended an international Internet Crimes Against Children Conference in Dallas, Texas, run by the Dallas Child Advocacy Center and the Crimes Against Children Division of the Collin County Criminal District Attorney's Office.

It was the first time I had been surrounded by detectives who carried out the same investigations I did — a brotherhood and sisterhood of 2,500 people who understood the issues Australian police experienced online. Related professions, including pastoral care

personnel, guidance counsellors, and prosecutors, covering a range of internet and physical world issues, attended the Dallas conference.

Our US colleagues could not have been more cooperative in showing us how they conducted their investigations, how they recorded online evidence, the programs they were using, and their relevant legislation. Unlike in Australia, US police need to establish that the child displayed in a seized video or photo is a real child before they can charge someone with possession of child pornography. That one seemingly small challenge makes their investigations difficult. They virtually need to produce the child victim, and that victim might no longer be a child.

Conversely, to gather and progress evidence in Australia, footage containing images of people who simply appear to be a child is an effective starting point to develop a case. Supportive legislation in Australia is a positive indication of the community wanting to stamp out this evil. It has given Australian police an advantage in what they are able to address.

However, when I left the police force, there was still widespread lack of understanding among police in both the US and Australia of the threat to children online. In my home state of Queensland, I was assigned to attend the police academy to make a presentation to plainclothes officers seeking to earn an appointment as detectives. I explained the online detective's role and how we carried out our work and could assist them with their investigations. A drug squad detective

scheduled to make a presentation just before me had asked organisers, 'You won't mind if I go a bit longer? The next presentation will be a bit boring. No one cares about what people are doing on the internet.' There was little comprehension that real-life people were grooming children online in real-life time. It was hard to convince many of my police colleagues that real crimes were being committed on the internet.

The police were not the only ones unconvinced of the value of online surveillance and the need to protect the vulnerable from a new breed of predator. The wider community was sceptical too, and even to the present day, many parents are still not on board. Accepting an invitation to take part in a government-run panel charged with discussing online child protection, I was shocked by a comment made by a panel member who was highly skilled in technical aspects surrounding the internet, including social media. With all good intentions, he asked, 'Is this really a problem? Are there really adults online trying to abuse children?'

Some people are still offended if I mention that the internet can create issues. They think I am attacking technology. Of course, I am not. E-learning and everything else that goes with internet use must work hand in hand with online safety education, awareness, and responsibility.

Growing numbers in the police and wider community are having their minds broadened to realise that the online threat is real. During my presentations at schools, I show the students' parents a chat between a

predator and a real child and many realise for the first time that the problem is tangible.

Mums and dads can play a significant role by becoming involved in safeguarding their children. It is not simply a matter for them to conclude the internet is bad. The good and bad aspects of the internet mirror the physical world, and just as parents protect their children with common sense in the physical world, they can be involved online.

Conversely, there is no place for paranoia towards the internet. We cannot be scared of the internet, because there is nothing to be scared of. It is not the medium that offends; it is the people who choose to use it wrongly. I have arrested dozens of people for pushing the wrong buttons on their keyboards. People are going to prison for doing that. When that happens, it brings home the message that the internet is not another world.

The internet is here to stay, and its positive uses are countless. In fact, it was responsible for the international ties established between the Crime and Misconduct Commission, the Queensland Police and the US law enforcement agencies.

Overcoming Ignorance — the Big Challenge to a Global Solution

- At an international level — a greater commitment to collaboration and communication between international, national, and regional agencies to fight this social evil.

- At a community level — acknowledging the seriousness of the issue and devoting an appropriate amount of resources and personnel to the task.

- At a personal level — educating children, their parents, and caregivers that online stalkers with wrong intentions exist and teaching them how to stay safe.

30
Internet Requires
a United Approach

Online cooperation between Australian law enforcement agencies gained traction long before I left the police force. Queensland was the first Australian state to effectively engage in online investigations. As the other states followed, the South Australian police approached us to train a unit so they, too, could investigate online and networked paedophilia. To put together a report to establish the unit, I investigated how prevalent predatory behaviour was online in South Australia and the type of inappropriate, illegal online activity that was happening in the region.

To assist police there, I assumed the fictitious identities of young people living in South Australia and began online investigations. The results astounded me. I had never identified so many predators on the internet as we found stalking South Australian children. The first time I logged into chat rooms or public forums specific to South Australia, so many inappropriate approaches were being made by adults to young people. It appeared to me the perpetrators had never considered their actions might be viewed or investigated by police, parents, or teachers. The number of adults detected in the first couple of hours

targeting or committing offences against children was overwhelming.

It took the team several days to gather evidence on online offenders located in South Australian capital Adelaide who were committing offences or indicating they wanted to meet their victims in person. This evidence was forwarded to local police to execute arrest warrants, and a South Australian online investigation unit was established. The answer had come back clearly to South Australia's question of whether a need existed in their state to create a unit. In fact, given the global nature of the internet, surveillance and education on safeguarding children is needed everywhere.

I sought support from a politician when I began training in schools. An older lady who had no children, said, 'I know there are criminals and predators on the internet because I have heard about it, but do you think it is a problem in our area?'

This mindset is dangerous — some people are stuck in the past in thinking internet issues that communities face are purely geographical. Predator behaviours, assaults on victims and inappropriate activity can occur anywhere in the world because human nature is the same everywhere and the internet is global in reach. A change of thinking is needed. The internet has brought the whole world together. Good influences by good people around the globe are now accessible in local communities. Conversely, a small percentage of

bad influences by bad people has also encroached and requires a change of mindset to address.

Queensland detectives anticipated predators would be active in South Australia when we were assigned to look for offenders there. We found they were using similar methodologies to those adopted by predators in my home state. They were behaving in the same way, requesting the same things from their victims. The internet has brought people together, and a change of approach is required to deal with global online issues.

Police and legal professions in Australia are still coming to terms with online offences. The seriousness of these offences and how they destroy people's lives are minimised by those who do not yet understand what, to them, is largely an invisible world. This is no indictment on these people. It took me being thrown in the deep end to experience the impact of an online predator on their victim. More evidence of the tragic consequences of this form of online crime is becoming public though. The impacts are only partially highlighted through media reports of adults and young people who have taken their lives after being cruelly treated on social networking sites. Issues created online nearly always manifest in the physical world.

Programs are run in prison to teach online offenders to realistically deal with their fantasies and understand the true impacts of their crimes. These courses are not compulsory; however, participating can result in a reduction in an offender's sentence.

I was involved in a trial where a judge admitted, 'I don't know much about this new internet thing,' to which we advised him that it had been around for about ten years. It is not just me who has learnt during my five years as an online investigator and the time since; the whole justice system has been evolving and learning. 'Real society' has been around for centuries and still does not and never will operate perfectly. We have not yet been around for the full life span of someone who was born and died since the advent of the digital world.

Queensland has led the way in Australia, and perhaps the world, in legislating to protect children online by introducing Section 218A to the Criminal Code. No real child needs to be involved. This legislation has been immensely helpful in enabling police to remove dangerous people from cyberspace, hopefully before offending against a real child. In 2005, four child exploitation material (CEM) offences were inserted in the Queensland Criminal Code:

- Involving a child in making CEM (s. 228A)

- Making CEM (s. 228B)

- Distributing CEM (s. 228C)

- Possessing CEM (s. 228D).

The 2013 Criminal Law Amendment Act increased the maximum penalty for the first three offences from

ten to fourteen years' jail and the maximum penalty for possession from five to fourteen years.

While involvement by police and other community experts is crucial to make the online playground safer for children, my overriding conviction is that the most important role will, and should be, played by parents.

Benefits of a United Approach

- Jurisdictions should cooperate and establish agreement on what is acceptable online.
- Australia and the United States are not alone in online enforcement initiatives. A Virtual Global Taskforce is very active. The ongoing challenges to its effectiveness are resourcing, time zones, and language.
- The ultimate answer is educating young people because they are otherwise powerless.
- More parents, schools, and communities are being empowered through education.
- Cooperation and shared learnings with welfare groups, technology groups, psychologists, and psychiatrists will be important in developing comprehensive support and educational networks.
- Parents are the biggest key to keeping children safe online.

31
Parents, You're the Key!

Parents often do not understand the nature of the internet — both its potential and its pitfalls — and so are reluctant to get involved. The type of parental involvement that makes a difference in the physical world is the very thing needed to make a difference online. The messages should never be overcomplicated. Most cyber-safety advice is straightforward. Even though it is simple, parental supervision of internet safety issues is powerful and most times essential.

The rewards for parents committed to applying their mindset and actions to guide their children's online development and protect them from the wrong influence are immeasurable.

At the same time, parents should take the pressure off themselves. No one is perfect, and adults and children are going to make mistakes online, the same as in the physical world. Every parent must accept that their son or daughter will make mistakes as they learn.

To prey on children, dangerous people go to where children frequent. They will pretend to be teenage girls or boys, or maybe trusted adults. Parents' presence in the online playground and putting the right measures in place will reduce the risks to nearly zero that their

children will fall victim to life-changing threats posed by predators.

By being engaged on this issue, parents are reducing the chances that dangerous people will access their children and, if they do, ensuring that access will not be ongoing. It is not about stopping children from using technology. It is about being there to make sure everything is okay.

A common-sense approach to online parenting will always be better than a technical approach. While using monitoring software and understanding the security features of sites children frequent will help, busy parents often struggle to keep up with the rapidly changing nature of technology. The current online technological solutions will be superseded within two to three years. On the other hand, common sense is never outdated.

In five years' time, young people will not use the programs they use now. As they get older, different things interest them. New forms of social media will replace many programs that are currently popular. When I began presenting in schools, teens used MSN Messenger, which had more functionality than Instagram or other popular messaging or micro-blogging sites. Four years later, every Australian teenager online used Myspace. No one used Facebook. They used to tell me, 'We will never use Facebook. That is for old people.' Then everybody changed. Yet Facebook does nothing different than Myspace used to do; both programs are identical in functionality.

Interacting with a child about their internet usage is far more important. Certain behaviours should alert suspicions. If the child says, 'I do not want you to see what I am doing on the internet,' they are really saying, 'Why would I not want you to see it? Why would I want to hide my screen from you? I am doing something wrong.' They are telling their parent, 'You really should take a look at my screen.'

It is also irrational for a young person to suggest that a parent showing an interest in their internet usage is 'invading my privacy' or 'like reading my diary'. Why? A diary is something that I keep to myself; communicating on the internet is the exact opposite — anything posted is shared with the whole world. The internet cannot guarantee privacy. Maybe that young person is saying to their parent, 'I am happy for everybody in the world to see what I am saying except for you.'

A parent does not need to see every message or look over their child's shoulder twenty-four hours a day, but they have a right to know where they are going and if they are okay.

I can tell by my children's facial expressions when I walk into the room whether they are looking at something on the screen that I should be concerned about. They are supposed to be having a good time online. If they look concerned, puzzled, confused, or withdrawn, I check with them whether anything is wrong. It is a tragedy when parents feel anxious and unsure in their own homes because they do not know what is happening behind a closed door. The first house

rule for responsible and safer use of technology is to keep the computer out of closed off rooms. It should only be used in public where other household members can freely see what it is being used for.

A Year 4 student once told me, 'Some of us were playing a game on the internet and someone asked me for my address.' 'Did you give it to them?' I asked. 'No,' the child said. 'Because my mum said that when I am playing games on the internet, I am not allowed to give out any of our family details.' If that young child had not been warned by her parent against giving her address out, she would not have known there was anything wrong with doing that. She heard from her mum that you do not share information on the internet.

That was simple and powerful parenting at work. It did not involve some wonderful new message or accessing better technology with built-in safeguards. It involved passing on a simple, basic message to the child that they heard over and over until the associated safeguards became a normal part of their cyber world. Parents do not need their children to agree with their decision on technology; they just want them to accept it.

Each family should find what works for them, taking into account their needs, children's personalities, and family dynamics. Considerations in determining family usage include:

1. Why are we spending so much time on it? What is it achieving? Is it producing anything?

2. Is it time or value friendly? Are we enjoying it?

3. Would our lives be more productive and happier if we did not use certain programs?

4. Do we feel that using a program is a necessity or just convenient, and what are the potential hazards and risks to us and our families?

A widespread fear among young people is that if they make a mistake or have a problem on the internet and tell their parents, they will lose technology. Their concern is not based on fact, as most parents know that technology is an integral part of their child's life.

When children face problems in the physical world, they go straight to a trusted adult. This same mindset can be created toward online issues.

There is not one program a child will want to use outside the school environment that is essential to their development, achievements, or health and wellbeing. All online social and gaming sites are optional extras and should be treated as such. Parents should not fall for the line 'all my friends are using it'. If they have a particular reservation about the programs their child is into, the chances are other parents are thinking the same thing.

When my children's friends come over to play or have a sleepover, every one of them automatically leaves their devices on our bench when they go to a bedroom or retire for the night. They may not understand why. It may

be different to the rules in their home, but they accept it. Would something bad happen if I let them use the devices in my children's bedrooms? Maybe not on that occasion, or maybe yes. I am just working at reducing the risks and potential issues. After taking this measure as a parent, it is a great feeling to fall asleep knowing that the children are sleeping and nobody outside the home can contact and communicate with them.

Are my children teased or targeted because they cannot use the internet in their bedroom? Absolutely not. It is crucial for parents to consider and always remember the following:

- Parents make the decisions, not technology.

- Parents have a right to be part of their child's online experience and to know who they are associating with and where they are going.

- Children need boundaries when technology is involved, the same as in every other aspect of their lives.

- Parents can create an open digital environment within the home that empowers their children to talk to them about online issues, mistakes, and problems. Parents can only help if they know.

- Parents can re-assure their children that something can always be done to solve online

issues, and if they open up about their problems, they will not lose technology.

Reducing the risks of online issues usually will not happen naturally. Parents can make it happen by being involved in their child's online experiences, acting on their convictions, and installing boundaries.

It is best to start educating and moulding a child to expected behaviours and expectations as soon as, if not before, they type one key; however, it is never too late. Once a parent truly understands the issues their child faces using technology are about morals, beliefs, ethics, boundaries, and expectations, they become empowered and perfectly positioned to know the decisions they should be making.

A parent can argue they cannot stop their child from taking their small technology devices, such as smart phones and iPods, into their bedroom. This is a defeatist attitude and no excuse for not monitoring their child's internet usage. Ground rules can still be put in place.

My daughter has an iPod, which she uses to chat to her friend. She has messaging software on it and is allowed to use it selectively to chat with some of her friends, but she is not allowed to take the iPod to her bedroom. In our home, smart phones are not to be used in the bedroom; that is one of our rules. My wife and I also model this behaviour.

If parents apply this principle, it will repay them in gold for the rest of their lives.

A parent does not need to look over their child's shoulder twenty-four hours a day for a predator to quickly learn that someone is watching out for their child's safety. The requirement to keep all internet usage out in the open is the best safeguard I know.

- Parent, you are the best line of defence — your child needs your life skills.
- Understand that online issues are real — not just data on a screen — and can affect any child.

32
Education Is Simple
and Essential

Education on online issues is critical to ensure young people are truly aware of the world they socialise in. I was taken aback the first time a Year 10 girl asked me why an adult man would want to have sex with her. I gathered my senses in time to respond, 'I do not know why. I just know that men with these wrong intentions exist.' The girl's disbelief and ignorance shocked me, with the realisation that many girls her age are not even on the lookout for stranger danger, either online or in the physical world. The evil intentions of dangerous people are not even thought about by their innocent and naïve targets. That is why young girls and boys are vulnerable. It is not that they are unintelligent or looking to do the wrong thing. They are children and are looking for something different online, not adults with wrong motives.

That interaction with the girl was a turning point in my understanding. It is not the last time I have heard girls and boys react with naïve bewilderment when warned of the dangers of strangers wanting to befriend them online. The experience triggered in me an acute awareness of the need for parents to actively monitor their children's online activity and

protect them from potential dangers. The aim of the resulting parental education is not to create fear, which is counterproductive. Rather, it is to highlight the truth so parents and their children have an accurate understanding of the world they are in.

While visiting a school with detective partners to make a presentation to students, I realised that teachers and students could benefit from knowledge I took for granted from my countless online interactions and investigations. I saw a sudden awareness light up their faces or at times an expression of shock as I talked about my online experiences. I found it incomprehensible that adults with wrong intentions could access these children online who were so naïve about how they operated.

The internet can be the safest place children will ever be, but ensuring their security will not happen by accident. Parents and the wider community must make it that way. In most homes, a small change of mindset is all that is needed to result in more responsible internet use by both parents and children. Parents need to acknowledge how much their children need their input and become committed to teaching them to make good online choices. This is not formal classroom teaching but rather passing on little keys that will ensure the health and wellbeing of children online. This mentoring is the responsibility of parents, support workers, other responsible adults and teachers

and should be coupled with a positive attitude towards technology.

It is easy to focus on those who are doing the wrong thing, but society should not be too overwhelmed by them. They are the minority no matter how it appears. Despite online detectives seeing an uglier face online than some people may care to imagine, parents should not be made to feel that every time their child goes online, a predator strike is imminent. Internet stalking is a small but very real part of the internet. The term 'low risk, high consequence' describes perfectly the online threat to children's safety. Parents should be involved in a relaxed way, but if they feel something is not right, take the right measures to deal with it.

Proactive education that is clear, concise, and consistent is the key. Keep the teaching simple. When teaching a child not to steal something, a parent is unlikely to say, 'You should not steal something because it is not good for the economy of Australia!' or, 'It is not good for the welfare of the shop keeper.' They simply say, 'You just do not steal things.' That is very simple. People cannot take something without permission, without authority. That is not the right thing to do.

Parents should keep the messages basic and simple. If more parents would grasp this, online safety education in schools and formal courses would become far more effective. Educators would simply need to reinforce the messages children already know because they have heard it from their parents. Inputs from parents can ensure that children possess the common sense,

having heard it both at home and at school. It is all about hearing the same basic, simple messages over and over and over.

Every day in real life parents teach their children the necessary skills to question the motives and behaviours of strangers. Teaching children to trust their instincts and make good choices online and in the physical world will open up doors for them, instead of bad choices that give people an opportunity to close doors. In making poor choices, they might let other people change the course of their lives. Recognising dangers, responsibilities, expectations and awareness does not come naturally; children must be taught. They must be alerted to the online dangers and responsibilities, understand the dangers are real, and be able to identify and avoid the risks. It is a matter of putting everyday skills to good use:

'Why would an online stranger want the information they are seeking?'

'Why would they want to hurt me or my family?'

Only a handful of people in their lives have the opportunity to effectively teach children these skills — parents, guardians, support workers, and teachers. It is unlikely that anyone else will be the safeguard and a filter between a child and every person or thing — good or bad — that vies for their attention online.

Online stalking is so rife that police detective work will never eliminate the problem, it can only help to reduce it. The key is education and eliminating the potential

victims rather than the perpetrators. Online policing is essential, and detectives do a magnificent job of potentially saving so many children, but their work is not the key to turning around this issue. Prevention through education is the best way.

Parenting on online issues will not always be easy. Making good choices regarding technology will not be popular. If children do not like some of the decisions their parents make about their internet usage, parents can take heart from knowing they are doing their job well. That is just part of being a parent.

Adults can take for granted the coping and problem solving skills and strategies they possess that help them deal with many and varied issues others create in their lives. Children and young people are still developing these skills and look at the world through different eyes. Parents can instil a belief in children, as they do in the physical world, that they have their best interests at heart and the means to help them solve their problems with others. Dilemmas that seem simple to an adult may not seem so to a young person.

I am constantly amazed by stories I hear from schools and individuals about how the issues ceased when they acted against cyber bullying in the physical world. Shining the light on the situation made far more of a difference than they ever imagined. Many students have told me they have been subjected to cyber bullying. When I ask what they have done to avoid the bullying or to recover, they invariably reply, 'Nothing.' When I ask why they believe nothing can be done to help, they have

to admit that this belief is not based on fact but on what they imagine. Some say they do not know the offender and that nothing can be done to locate the person.

One teen boy told me the perpetrator went to another school, so nothing could be done. 'Maybe no one would take it seriously,' he said in a defeated tone. 'Maybe it is my fault. I encouraged it or may have been a part of it myself.' Whatever the excuses, the result was the bullying continued. It increased and the problems compounded.

Parents should communicate clearly with children that something can be done to help with any problem they face with technology. If they do not hear these words from their parents, they will not hear them from anyone. Parents must firmly believe something can always be done. If the first strategy does not work, move on. Even if a person attacking a child is never located, a parent's intervening actions can still cause the bullying to cease. Children must be taught that something can always be done to help.

Leave it up to a sixteen year old boy, and he will watch television until 2 a.m. every morning on a school night. That is not because he is a bad kid, but because he cannot see anything wrong with that. A parent looks at the world from a different perspective and puts in place bedtimes. They also require the boy to put time aside for his homework. The passion to parent diligently can also be adopted when it comes to technology. If a parent trusts their instincts and does it for the benefit of their child, it will be a sound decision.

I have had people say to me, 'Oh, you are an IT expert. I work in IT.' I reply, 'I am not an IT expert. I am an expert in knowing how to successfully be a part of the cyber-environment.' For generations parents have been making good choices, determining boundaries, responsibilities, and what is and is not acceptable. All that is needed is to transfer that knowledge and the accompanying skills to helping their children use technology.

Every parent can play a part in their child's education, not only academically, but also in passing on life skills. If children know they have online rules, rights, and regulations, and that the online communication they engage with is real, they will have a better internet experience. Teach them to manage technology, or it will manage them.

The following fundamentals form a solid basis for online parenting:

1. The internet is a great world. It is a safe world. It is going to give children opportunities pre-internet generations could only dream of. Before the internet, children growing up at primary school had the library. When they were learning, say, about Japan, only one book in the library written about sixty years earlier could help. Today children can get on the internet and communicate with children their own age in a school in Japan. The internet can be used to expand people's minds. It is a great and a safe world. Never blame the technology.

2. Children need to be part of the internet world. Gone are the days when it was an option. When children leave the educational environment, very few jobs or activities they will be engaged in will not involve being part of the cyber experience. When they get a job, or go to college or university, they will need to access the internet. If they take a gap year and travel the world, they will still need to know how to be part of the cyber environment. What better time to teach them than now?

3. Parents already possess the required life skills and adult instincts. Children should not be handed technology without learning lessons or having boundaries put in place until they are adults. If they are left to their own devices, they are going to make all the silly mistakes some adults are making in the physical world right now because they were not mentored when they were younger. Children know how to use technology in a physical sense — how to type, swipe, and push buttons — however they must be taught the full implications of what it means to take part in responsible digital communication and sharing of information. Their minds have not yet been conditioned to understand what this is really all about. Changing the mindset — even slightly — of a young technology user who may think they know it all but still need guidance is the influence that good parenting can have.

4. Parents must be engaged in their children's internet journey. Hand a child aged five, six, seven, eight, nine, or ten a device that is internet enabled without instructions, supervision, or rules, and they will have real issues. It has got nothing to do with how smart or otherwise a child is or how good or bad they are. They will be children. Further, parents cannot control everybody else out in the cyber world or how they are going to interact with their child. They can just put in place the correct measures to ensure a safer journey for their child.

The four things a parent should believe:

| The Internet is a great world | Children need to be part of the Internet | Parents already possess the required skills | Parents must be engaged in their child's internet journey |

33
It Takes the Whole 'Village'

The African proverb, 'It takes a village to raise a child' rings true when putting forward the best approach to address internet issues. I was invited to join in a round table session hosted and chaired by an Australian Federal Opposition working group looking at internet safety and cyber bullying strategies. Community members from different disciplines were invited. The group established that young people are experiencing issues in their lives entirely or partially owing to interactions on the internet or mobile phones. It also concluded that education was the most effective answer to the issues. Although a good starting point, the conclusion is a starting point only. A holistic, community-changing solution is needed.

Working with more than 100,000 students, teachers, and parents a year at more than 150 schools throughout Australia and New Zealand, I am immersed in internet safety and cyber bullying education. The conclusions came as no surprise. Education is the key. A holistic educational process to protect the online community is possible and achievable. The educational environment is the forum to address the challenge, and parents are the most important influence on children putting what they learn into practice.

Schools are the ideal setting to teach young people safe use of electronic communication because they do not get to use technology in their bedrooms. Schools create a very realistic environment involving real people, a public setting in which young people's online activity is monitored and they are held accountable. Young people can be taught to handle technology appropriately.

Technology and its rapid expansion are not the concern. The flow-on social issues are. How they are created or surface during internet use needs to be addressed. Children are being introduced to the internet at increasingly younger ages, and more elderly people are using it too. Options to socialise online are multiplying. Gadgets to access the internet are becoming cheaper. More schools are introducing technology to children of all ages. More places provide internet access. The more people use technology, the more issues surface. The internet has changed the social framework of society, and communities must adapt. Cyber education needs to be prioritised and integrated into education as passionately and automatically as traditional teaching requirements. The internet offers children so much and can be used to create, produce, entertain, and socialise. As with every aspect of their lives, young people can be educated to identify risk and danger, protect themselves and respect others.

Communities have long emphasised teaching skills so young people can assimilate into the physical world productively and avoid danger, trouble, and embarrassment. Acknowledging that the internet is

a crucial part of the real world in which real people interact with real people, and deal with the same issues as in the physical world, brings an appreciation of the need for teaching on sensible internet usage.

The issues people face online involve serious physical world responsibilities. People sitting in the privacy of their homes, typing keys, are committing criminal offences. Many are sitting in prison for downloading the wrong types of images. This makes internet safety and cyber bullying education essential. Holistic solutions must be reached from the many forums held to discuss the topic. When young people log into the digital world, there will always be a risk of them being confronted by issues. The risks can be minimised by educating them to trust what they have been taught and to listen to their instincts.

Sceptics assume internet safety and cyber bullying education is the enemy of technology, designed to make users paranoid and stop them using technology. In fact, this form of education has the opposite effect. It enables educated users to embrace being a part of the digital world by reducing the risks they face. As soon as a child starts using technology, they need to be taught to identify risks, be aware of rights and responsibilities, and protect themselves. If they are not taught early, they will not learn in time for when they need it most. A parent would never wait until their child is thirteen to teach them to wear a seatbelt. The teaching occurs as soon as the child begins travelling in a vehicle. Handing a digital appliance to a child without educating them on

its proper use is like handing a set of car keys to a sixteen year old without lessons or knowledge of road rules.

Individuals, groups, and organisations worldwide have begun addressing the need for education. The influence they are already having needs to be promoted more widely. I constantly receive feedback from students and parents that my presentations have made a difference to their families. While this is satisfying, the messages are not getting out to enough families. A holistic shift in community mindset and behaviour regarding technology will only occur when teaching is prioritised. Then all of society will be the winner.

No single strategy will be the answer. The solution should include varying forms of teaching. More than one library book is used to teach a child about World War II. Publications with varying views and information are accessed, along with other methods, such as in-class education, projects, online research, attending ANZAC day parades, speaking with those involved in the conflict, documentaries, and at-home education. Cyber safety education should be approached the same way.

Internet safety presentations in schools make a difference, but my sessions are just one string in the bow. They cannot change behaviours on their own. Schools are also very active in internet education and need more support and structure to make a real difference. No one person, group, or organisation — private or government — can change how young people use or perceive technology in a holistic sense.

Internet safety and cyber bullying education should be made fun, accessible, and relevant to each age group. To achieve this, the relevant education should start in primary school. A school I visited had just one computer per student three years ago; it now supplies a laptop to every Year 5 student. Things are changing rapidly, and education needs to adapt accordingly.

Schools are an ideal venue to train students, teachers, and parents as they embrace technology and would provide a fantastic hub to address internet safety. Students' education might include pattern matching/ monitoring programs where correct choices align with responsible online behaviours.

Training teachers is essential as they will largely coordinate strategies to educate students in online safety. They have children as their captive audience during school hours and, generally, have a lot of credibility.

Parental education about internet safety is paramount, and the challenge is getting this instruction to as many parents as possible. The only way to achieve holistic change is to make this education compulsory. It must become an accepted part of a parent's responsibility when they have a child in school. Some schools are already making parents' internet education a condition of enrolment or before their child can be issued a digital device at school. It may hurt for the first few years, but eventually will become accepted.

Knowledge is never automatically gained without experience or education. Parents attending my sessions

learn small, effective changes to implement at home. They are grateful and often tell me they now view technology differently.

Other options are available for time-poor parents. I run ongoing education with a 24-school cluster representing 16,000 families where parental education is delivered via web-based resources and courses on: http://www.internetsafeeducation.com.

A typical session for parents might outline cyber safety messages being given to children so that these can be reflected in the home. Schools that have implemented compulsory parental education report the parents feel unity and solidarity when they see other parents have attended and heard the message. They are not on their own.

Making it compulsory gives the education credibility. Parents learn rights and responsibilities expected from their children. They learn where the school stands and what is expected from them as parents. They see solutions and strategies offered by the school. They learn they do not need extensive internet technology skills, just parenting skills. They learn their involvement is imperative and become confident they can make a difference. The students see the school and parents are on the same page and united. Children want boundaries, but these need to be consistent. Holistic education leads to this. A key to positive change is simple, consistent messages that are delivered differently and repeatedly:

In-class — Handouts, discussion, reflection, and projects.

Online — Age-appropriate online courses containing fun, interactive, and age-specific topic modules with clearly constructed learning outcomes.

External — Stand and deliver, theatre, webinars, and music programs that reflect the messages taught in school and consolidate the learning.

School-based — Acceptable user agreements/policies and school-/home-based pattern matching and monitoring software.

In-home — Parents reflecting school-based education in the home through rules, guidelines, consequences, communication, expectations, and family ethics, complemented by the optional use of parental filtering and/or monitoring software.

34
What Are the Impacts
on Young Minds?

Ongoing research can provide communities with valuable insights into the long-term effects of child exploitation materials on young people. Just a few questions based on my own observations:

Are some online interactions damaging children's emotions and, if so, how?

During a classroom session at a private girls' school, I was taken aback at the response when I asked thirteen year old students, 'How did that make you feel?' about certain things they read online. They did not respond with how it made them feel. They could only relate 'what was happening'. These girls seemed to be finding it very difficult to internalise the internet's impacts.

It appears that some young internet users are becoming traumatised emotionally. In the physical world, it is not uncommon for someone who has witnessed a traumatic event to comment, 'I felt numbed.' Yet my observation is that some young people cannot even verbalise how they feel when encountering certain issues online. Is an epidemic of emotional damage occurring to children right under the noses of parents who are barely aware of it?

How and why do online words and imagery deceive so easily?

As an exercise with young students I play a video depicting an online cartoon based game designed for children aged six to twelve. The program's software translates members' keyed-in communications into the actions of cartoon characters. Every user playing that game is running around in that world as their own character. I then tell children, 'There is a pink character called Emma. Can anyone describe to me the type of person who may be controlling that character at the other end?'

Most perceive the pink cartoon character as non-threatening and respond with, 'Oh, she is probably nice, just like me.'

One student said, 'Oh, she is an adult. She could be someone that wants to take me away. She could be nasty. She could be a cyber-bully.' Having been taught online stranger danger, this student is more discerning but still assumes the person behind a 'pink' character is a woman.

Where do children get these perceptions? They almost always say the pink character is a 'she'. Their minds have already convinced them that the person controlling that character is a girl.

Then someone gets smart and says, 'She could be a man.'

The pink character could be any of these scenarios. Most often, the person behind the character in this child's site is harmless, but online detectives sometimes

learn that the background person is more sinister — not nice, and invariably not female. This online role-playing game illustrates how someone hiding behind the anonymity of a screen can deceive a child, manipulating the innocent and naïve into believing they are someone they are not. It is a perfect example of the screen's powerful effect on a young person's mind.

Take the example I mentioned earlier of the boy who learnt the girl I was pretending to be did not exist and that he was talking to me in disguise. Yet he still responded with, 'She knows my name. She knows where I live.' I was stunned that he still referred to me as 'she' one minute after learning who I was.

Insights and awareness in this area need to filter into the education system and the public domain to help society educate children to be aware of the dangers of making online assumptions.

What are the impacts of ever-increasing access to online information on younger minds?

Safeguarding children online should extend to monitoring how the pace at which the internet is expanding impacts them. Is it forcing them to grow up earlier?

A sixteen year old at a boys' school shared how he met a 'teenage girl' on Facebook. 'She' went to a different school in town. They agreed to meet in person. His eleven year old mate saw the girl's profile and said, 'That is dodgy. Something is not right.' It turned out that the younger friend was right to be suspicious. The older boy could not see that. He fell in love with the girl

on the internet. It took his friends to point out to him a few things about the girl's profile that did not add up.

Why do online abuse victims feel compelled to revisit the point of their pain?

Victims of severe online bullying have told me how they read the offending posts over and over again. I struggled to understand why they felt compelled to visit a site where others were cruel to them. Then in the course of my online policing, I viewed a video clip of extreme real-life violence that I found deeply disturbing. It bothered me, and I found myself thinking about the scene more than was healthy. Like the victims of bullying, I felt drawn to watch the video again. I have since wondered why.

Maybe I wanted to view it again in the hope that I overreacted and it really was not as bad the second time. Perhaps my self-assessment provides a clue to why victims of bullying continue to punish themselves. Are they hoping each time they read a cruel post that it is not as hurtful as they first thought? After revisiting the site that disturbed me, I learnt I recoiled the way I did the first time for a reason and the site again served no positive purpose. I now avoid revisiting material or conversations of that nature. What is heard and seen can be as damaging as physical assault and battery.

Generally, people do not want to stay in the place where they feel bad, others are attacking them, or they feel unsafe. Having spoken with thousands of teenagers, it is not uncommon to hear, 'I am using such and such a program. People are bullying me. What can I do?'

Adults may find this difficult to understand and say, 'Get out of the program.' This is easier said than done for young people. Children tell me they need to stay there so they can see what is being said about them or whether things will get better. Sadly, by staying there, the negative effects are compounded. Common sense suggests: Why would things change or get better?

Negative posts online are perhaps the present day equivalent of graffiti in the school toilets, one difference being that they have a wider audience. The posts say something about the narcissistic element of a generation that seems to think everyone cares about their every thought. Parents must empower children to take control and avoid activity or programs that have a negative effect on them. When I ask these children if they like feeling bad or unsafe, they answer, 'No.' When I ask them to consider why they are staying in a place they do not like, they generally see my reasoning. If negative online activity has seriously affected a child or family and the child is struggling to remove themselves from exposure to the offending content in a program, parents may have to take action. No program is worth the health and wellbeing of children. Children are letting others control them by staying in a program. Something can always be done to help, and more research could aid this.

What are the long-term effects of child exploitation material on the victim?

There is evidence to support the growing opinion that children abused through child exploitation material

will struggle more to have closure than children who have suffered sexual abuse in the physical world. This is not to downplay the severity or tragedy of either crime. From my observations investigating child exploitation in the physical world and online, I believe online abuse carries an additional sting to its tail.

The physical offence was committed at a physical place and point in time, and boundaries and knowledge relating to the offence can be worked on. The victim has a starting point to recover from once the offender is apprehended and punished. In contrast, children whose abuse has been recorded and posted online are being abused over and over and are unable to manage or control the abuse. The abuse has no end point. Even if the material is totally removed from existence, the victim will never know this. They fall into an abyss of the unknown where the crime and its effects are magnified in their minds.

Specialist therapies and treatments may be required to assist the victims. As community understanding grows, the severity of online offences may lead to harsher penalties for offenders. In her report, 'Overview of Federal Child Pornography Issues' in the Texas BarCLE on January 10 and 11, 2013, Camille E. Sparks from the US Attorney's Office in the Northern District of Texas indicates this:

> As more is learnt and measured about the impacts of online sex offences against children, it could be that online production, distribution, possession of child pornography pictures and videos could result in significantly more severe penalties than in the physical world.

Why: The offence has occurred to the child in production, as in the physical world. But that offence has continued on through the distribution and multiple viewing online. In the physical world, when an offender offends against a child, there is one child victim; when an offender distributes or views hundreds of child pornography images or videos there are countless videos. This is why the penalty needs to be harsh.

While individuals continue to buy, view, collect, use, and distribute child exploitation material, they are creating demand for it. For this material to be created, a child needs to be abused. While there is a demand for these materials to be created, shared, used, and possessed, children will continue to be abused. This material, when used by adults in particular, will fuel their unlawful sexual desires towards children. For some, this abuse is a very profitable business. Individuals who do not produce child exploitation material but have a demand for it are actively and illegally encouraging the abuse of children. It has got to stop being treated like data and material. This material should never be trivialised.

Should more severe penalties be introduced for online offenders?

When discussing child exploitation material, some people have the idea that 'a few rude photos' is all that is at stake. However, this dismissive attitude was conclusively rebutted on February 15, 2012, in the US when Michele Collins, Vice President of the Exploited

Children Division and Assistant to the President of the National Center for Missing and Exploited Children (NCMEC), testified before the Sentencing Commission concerning federal child pornography offences.

Ms Collins reported that the most frequently submitted images of identified victims in the previous five years revealed the kind of sexual abuse most often depicted in the images. Obscenities by percentage depicted in the series were as follows:

- 84% oral sex

- 76% anal and/or vaginal penetration

- 52% use of foreign objects or sexual devices

- 44% bondage or sado-masochism

- 20% urination and/or defecation

- 4% bestiality.

Ms Collins told the Commission sexual abuse victims suffer depression, withdrawal, anger, feelings of guilt, and responsibility for the abuse. She said it is impossible to know how often an image is viewed online and traded, but every time an image is downloaded or traded, the child is re-victimised.

One child victim, now an adult, is quoted: 'When I was told how many people have viewed these images

and videos I thought my pulse would stop. Thinking about all those sick perverts viewing my body being ravished and hurt like that makes me feel like I was raped by each and every one of them.'

The online pornography children risk being exposed to goes far beyond photos of naked men or women. Images and videos online go to the most depraved reaches of morality — bondage, bestiality, child abuse, fetishes, and other disturbing behaviours and practices. There are no limits. As a parent and layman adult, I cannot conceptualise how viewing this material would not leave an imprint on a developing child's mind.

This would not only desensitise or normalise the content, but it could very easily leave a permanent imprint in a child's memory. A detective, in my official role, I was required to view thousands of images and videos depicting the sexual abuse of children. To this day some of those images are still burned into my memory, occasionally popping up when I least expect. Society must never become complacent and pass this content off as just something children are exposed to these days.

Calls are growing stronger for harsher penalties based on the impacts. Just how serious the impacts are on young victims and the treatment thereof requires further investigation.

Knowing the law is an advantage; however, there is no substitute for proactive and common sense parenting.

35
Summing Up, Five Core
Steps for Parents

Five core steps are all parents need to know to model technology in family life for children from age five to late teens. The rewards for following my closing advice include less family conflict and avoiding the dangers and consequences other families may have to face and deal with. These simple steps will reduce online risks and potential issues to virtually zero. Never overcomplicate the process. It is not preventing children from using technology, rather it is helping them be a part of that world and making it safer for them.

Safeguard 1 — Parents, Take Charge
You are the one who controls technology and make the final decisions.

This is not about 'mistrusting' children; it is about acknowledging they are children, that they look at the world through different eyes and may not make the choices that are needed. As children grow, parents can let them make choices with less guidance but ensure their choices remain consistent with family requirements. The main decisions parents need to make surround:

- When technology is used

- Where technology is used

- What programs, apps, and sites are allowable

- With whom a child can connect with.

Don't allow technology to take charge. Do not believe that a program or website's popularity, user numbers, or profitability gives it credibility or suitability.

Safeguard 2 — Use Parental Controls

Parents have a right to know where their children go and who they communicate with.

Most schools have software or programs designed to monitor online activity. They do this because they have a duty of care for students. Parents also should have systems in place. Parents whose family have been devastated by online issues would now use monitoring or filtering software if they could turn back time and detect a potential problem early. They have told me so.

There will be those who claim this is 'spying' on children, as though parents are doing something wrong. Am I spying on my teenage daughter because I want to know where she is going with her friends on Friday night and who will be there? Of course not. I need to know this to make sure she is safe. When children become adults, they will not harbour a grudge; they will thank their parent for caring enough to monitor their activity, and most likely do the same with their children.

Parental controls work on a device or account to monitor or control information or activity. A variety of programs are available and some can be downloaded free. Functions that are more common include:

- Blocking concerning websites

- Setting time limits and ensuring curfews

- Recording websites visited

- Recording conversations in certain programs

- Limiting the downloading of particular apps

- Notifying a parent of concerning activity.

If parents start using monitoring or filtering programs early, it will become a part of their child's online world. They will be accustomed to it at home, just as they can expect to encounter it at school and then in the workplace.

Warning — Filtering or monitoring software should never be relied on as a total solution or a replacement for broader parental oversight.

Safeguard 3 — Stay Current
Parents should increase their knowledge base as needed.

This does not mean staying current with all technology, only technology relevant to the family.

Parents of five year old children do not necessarily need to know about Facebook yet. Staying current does not require parents becoming technology experts. It involves being across what children generally do on the internet, staying current by learning:

- What devices can connect to the internet

- When those devices are connected

- Where kids are going online and what programs and games they are using

- Who they are connected to.

Parents stay current by talking to their children and other adults, seeking advice, or asking questions from teachers and schools, and seeking information online.

Safeguard 4 — Set Rules and Boundaries

These are not optional.

Parents and children have rules and boundaries in every area of their lives. Rules don't stop them having fun; they protect them from themselves and others. Parents can be confident they are making a difference by putting rules in place. Rules can be changed if it is found they don't suit. As children grow, parents should not be afraid to modify a rule, taking care not to move outside their values, beliefs, morals, and ethics. Rules and boundaries provide security, letting children know where they stand.

The rules must be enforced or there is no point having them. They will not be taken as seriously if they can be continually broken unchallenged. On the other hand, it is not weakness to allow a couple more minutes playing a game.

General rules might include:

- Time limits and curfews

- An understanding of what language is acceptable

- Guidelines on where in the home technology can and can't be used

- What websites, games, and apps can be used

- What to do if something of concern happens or a mistake is made.

Safeguard 5 — Communicate

Create an environment of openness about technology and talk about it with your kids.

This is one strategy every parent can achieve and is the most important and effective safeguard against online issues. It is powerful to tell children, 'If you have a problem on the internet, or even if you make a mistake, I want you to talk to me about it and I promise I will help you solve the problem so you can keep having a good time online.'

Healthy communication about technology occurs by seizing the opportunities:

- Take ten minutes each day during school drop-off or pick-up.

- If you notice an unusual facial reaction after looking at a screen, ask what was that all about and is everything okay.

- Have a chat around the dinner table about what's happening online.

- Direct children to and discuss media articles about technology.

- Take other times to chat to children about what is happening online.

- Never underestimate the value of face-to-face communication. Research has shown that families who sit around a dinner table at least three times a week and talk are less likely to experience cyberbullying. The child ends up with a real feeling of support. If a child sex offender approaches them online and learns that their parents know about what happens on the internet, they will not hang around. As children grow, the way parents communicate with them changes. When they are young, parents 'tell' them; as

children move into their teens, the tone changes more to discussing, guiding, and suggesting.

- Parents should never stop communicating. They should talk to their children, other parents, friends, family, and school teachers.

Finally — Access These Practical Online Tools
As parents in general are time poor, the following resources provide practical advice and tools to help in the journey. Four 30-minute courses accessed through the website http://www.internetsafeeducation.com are designed for parents and carers to step you through what is needed to create that safe, happy, fun, and productive online environment. They are time-effective, up-to-date, and achievable, effectively addressing issues faced by families with young children through to young adults.

Core messages for the various age groups are:

- Start early, creating good habits and building a foundation (ages five to eight).

- Develop good decision making in the cyber world, providing guidance and rules (ages nine to eleven).

- Recognise the consequences and build responsible practices for secretive and savvy teens (ages thirteen to fourteen).

- Guide responsible adult decisions, being future focused (ages fifteen to eighteen).

Each course contains information, tools, links and videos and can be revisited, used, and shared indefinitely. http://www.internetsafeeducation.com is a one-stop shop containing regular blogs from myself and other authorities, and advice and tools to keep parents up to date with what they need to know.

Further valuable resources: http://www.nsteens.org and https://www.esafety.gov.au.

Mum and Dad, grandparents, teachers, guardians, and mentors, you hold the key to making the internet a far safer playground for your children. I hope this book empowers more of you to achieve that.

Remember, parents, you do not have to do much, but you must do something.